GROWING
UP
ON
TELEVISION

A REPORT TO PARENTS

GROWING UP ON TELEVISION

THE TV EFFECT

KATE MOODY

INTRODUCTION
BY NORMAN COUSINS

Times
BOOKS

Published by TIMES BOOKS, a division of
Quadrangle/The New York Times Book Co., Inc.
Three Park Avenue, New York, N.Y. 10016

Published simultaneously in Canada by
Fitzhenry & Whiteside, Ltd., Toronto

Library of Congress Cataloging in Publication Data

Moody, Kate.
Growing up on television.

Bibliography: p. 223
Includes index.
1. Television and children.
2. Children—United States. I. Title.
HQ784.T4M58 1980   791.45′01′3   79-91674
ISBN 0-8129-0902-X

Manufactured in the United States of America

Designed by Sharen DuGoff

TO
Bill and Scott and John

ACKNOWLEDGMENTS

I am most thankful for those who have offered information and insight—whether in real life, through books, or via television. I am especially grateful for the participation of the late Dr. Dorothy H. Cohen, psychologist and senior professor at Bank Street College of Education in New York City, who was never too busy to share her perceptions and care about this book.

Another brilliantly intuitive kindergarten teacher, Alison Stopford, has spent countless hours over the years relating classroom experiences with children and all media.

Kay Amicone gave valuable assistance as researcher, organizer of the manuscript, and contributor to several chapters. John Moody and Scott Moody were always willing to review TV programs, collect interviews from their peers, read manuscript, and offer opinions. Bill Moody, my husband, gave useful criticism throughout.

This book would not have occurred in its present form without Roger Jellinek, the Times editor who liked my ideas from the start. He steered the project creatively, offering me confidence, counselling—and deadlines!

Thoroughness, accuracy, and interpretation are always a concern. To the best of my ability I have studied and reported facts accurately and put what I learned into a reasonable conceptualization. Where I have made judgments and recommendations about personal uses of TV at home, it is in a spirit of creative assertiveness and experimentation rather than as an "authority" or "expert." The models for TV use which I suggest here may not be those that you would create for yourself; you will determine what works for you. It is my

general belief that in whatever way a person might use
television after he has given the matter careful thought, *that*
way will be better than it would have been without such
thought. My purpose, then, is to promote thinking about what
it means to grow up on television.

Kate Moody
Larchmont, New York
November 27, 1979

Introduction

BY

NORMAN COUSINS

For years the question has been debated whether the school or the family is the primary force in the education of the young. This question is academic. [Neither parents nor teachers are any longer the principal shaper of children's minds in the United States. Television is.]

A. L. Rowse, the English historian, once wrote that all the great changes in history have one theory in common: The people caught up in those changes never really know what is happening to them. Television became the most pervasive force in American life so quickly that its saturating effects have never really been comprehended. True, dozens of studies on the impact of television have been undertaken in the past quarter-century, but the full significance of TV as the central preoccupation of family life has yet to be assessed.

Kate Moody's *Growing Up on Television* throws a grand loop around all these separate reports and inquiries. In doing so, she has brought into clear view the wide range of problems resulting from the almost universal use of a new medium that is shaping the human mind to a far greater extent than any other instrument or institution in our history.

I had the privilege, in the 1950's and 1960's, of serving on the board of National Educational Television and, for a time, of being its chairman. NET helped to bring local noncommercial stations into being across the country and to furnish them with quality programming, however imprecise that term was and still is. The national activities of NET, especially on the programming level, were then privately supported. It was inevitable that the growth of noncommercial broadcasting could be sustained ultimately only through tax dollars. This development was marked by the creation of an umbrella body, known as the Corporation for Public Broadcasting, which served both as the conduit for public funds and as the prime integrator of all the various units and elements involved in nonprofit television.

⌊In those early years, we were animated by a vision of TV as a powerful instrument for nourishing and potentiating the human mind. We saw it in many roles—as a magnificent extension of the classroom, all the way from preschool day care centers to the university; as a source of competent news and information; as a home cultural center that would produce a harvest of great drama, books, and music; and, finally, as an arena for public debate and for the development of democratic institutions, giving the American people direct access to their public officials and to candidates for public office.⌋ HA HA

As we pursued this vision, however, we were aware that we were in a race against time in the sense that viewing habits were fast being formed by the American people. Many of these habits were being pre-empted by commercial TV, with more of everything—channels, dollars, fast-moving cameras, and high velocity content. It was also a race *for* time, in the sense that the channels that were to supply TV time to the American people were being snapped up—inevitably and understanda-bly—for commercial purposes. There were only so many channels to go around, and the federal government was giving away billions of dollars in TV air rights. Once having acquired a channel as a virtual gift, the recipient could turn around and sell the gift for millions of dollars. It will be contended that the recipient also incurred obligations and liabilities. True, he had to put up money for sophisticated equipment and facilities. He had to mount a programming capability. He had to demon-strate that he was allocating a certain amount of time to public information and public service. Granted. But the fact remains that all the exotic equipment and other capital expenditures accounted for only a fraction of the value of the franchise itself. And the franchise could be sold arbitrarily for many millions of dollars. Never in history was there a public giveaway to compare with it.

Even more appalling than the giveaway aspect was the fact that, in its haste to give away television channels to commercial broadcasters, the federal government short-changed noncommercial broadcasting, now known as public television. For example, in the nation's largest viewing market—the New York metropolitan area—no channels were reserved by the federal government for public broadcasting. The only way 12 million people in the New York area could obtain a channel was by *buying* a commercial station. Thus, Channel 13, acquired originally at virtually no cost from the American people, could be used for public broadcasting only at a cost of more than seven million dollars. The hero of that particular undertaking was Governor Robert Meyner of New Jersey who, against the natural protests of that state's business community—Channel 13 was New Jersey's only TV station and was needed for commercial purposes—supported the transfer of Channel 13 to a citizens' group. A large portion of the purchase money came not from the federal government but from the Ford Foundation.

All these facts are just a reflection of the reality that the society never thought through the entire television phenomenon. We didn't think through the implications of a device that would shape the contours of the American mind as it had been shaped by no other communication medium and possibly by no other institution, not excluding education or the Church. We haven't thought through the connection between the welter of images that are put into the human mind and their effect on the way the human mind functions, especially during the formative years. We haven't thought through the long-term effects on children of six hours of television viewing daily—the effects of rapid-fire picture changes; the effects of discontinuation and fragmentation of ideas, thoughts, and feelings; the effects of unremitting violence and the corresponding desensitization.⌋

The value of Kate Moody's book is that it enables the American people to do some long-overdue thinking. Mrs. Moody has assembled the pertinent facts and has set them down in a way that could lead to broad remedial action. Make no mistake about it, the material in this book is more than mere information; it is an explosion in the mind. It is difficult to imagine that anyone concerned about the essential well-being of this society will not be impelled to act upon Mrs. Moody's analyses and her eminently practicable suggestions.

CONTENTS

GROWING
UP
ON
TELEVISION

▪ 1 ▪

GROWING UP
ON
TELEVISION

Growing up on television is a new human condition. Never before has an entire generation been weaned by an electronic box and raised while spending so much of its waking time *watching*. What are the cumulative effects of habitual TV viewing? What can and should we do about them? This book addresses these questions.

My generation is the last—ever—to be raised primarily on print; none that comes after will have been so rooted in print, yet so exposed to television. Because of our unique perspective, our generation has the special assignment of teaching the young how to use television wisely. In the midst of a media revolution, it is especially important that we appreciate the values of print culture and try to incorporate them in those of the TV culture. But no future generation will understand so fully what this might mean.

I am sure that if we choose to we can still take charge of the TV revolution; yet we seem to have avoided the issue, and probably because we were raised in the "language of words" we are ineffectively ambivalent about television's power.

Nevertheless, we cannot ignore certain basic facts. The first is that the typical American child now watches television for more than 30 hours a week—that's more time than he spends with his parents, playing with peers, attending school, or reading books. When television first became available to consumers in about 1950, viewing was not a daily activity for most people. The first explosion of the television revolution came in the decade between 1950 and 1960 when the number of sets in use jumped 1,200 percent—from 4 million to 53 million in the United States. By 1960 the typical household was using a TV set five hours a day. By 1965 almost every home had TV and many had multiple sets.[1]

By 1970, 88 million sets were in use in the United States, and today there are no less than 144 million sets in this country (more TVs than telephones or bathtubs). Most families have several, placed in all of the key areas of the home: the living room, family room, kitchen, bedrooms—and the kids' rooms. TV sets are also found in classrooms, airports, restaurants, churches, and school cafeterias. In thirty short years—or one generation—the world has been swamped with television equipment and transformed by millions of television receivers and constellations of satellites and cables.

In the typical American household a TV set is turned on for six and a half hours a day—and this figure will increase in the 1980's, according to Frederick S. Pierce, president of ABC television, who says that "because of the energy problem and inflation, people are going to be spending more and more time before the set for entertainment, information and news. With gas prices continuing to rise, people are going to stay home more. It's possible, too, that business will go to a four-day work week to conserve energy."

While each member of the household is not glued to the screen for all of that time, some viewers are more persistent than others. Generally, the heaviest viewing groups are women, Blacks, the elderly, and children. Boys aged four to seven tend to be the most tenacious and stubborn viewers of all and are more vulnerable to the negative effects associated with such viewing than are girls. Babies start watching TV as early as three months old, often because their mothers feed them while they are watching soap operas or talk shows. The infants are drawn to the color and movement and sound coming from the screen and tend to watch this rather than mother's face or their own hands—as babies have heretofore

done. When they are about two years old, toddlers are led to
Sesame Street by parents who select this program because they
know that it is one of the few that is designed with children's
needs in mind; likewise *Mister Rogers' Neighborhood* and
Captain Kangaroo.[2]

While it is widely recognized that *Sesame Street* has been
able to teach children numbers and letters via TV entertainment, it is not generally realized how rapidly youngsters
outgrow *Sesame* and *Mister Rogers'*. By the age of four they are
already moving on to other channels, taking their addiction to
TV with them. Most of what these children then see is
produced in a commercial television system where impersonal
sex and violence prevail because they are the easiest means to
attract a large audience and sell profitable products on a mass
scale. This medium which can teach numbers and letters also
teaches how to execute a karate kick or use a handgun.

By the time children enter kindergarten most are averaging
more than 30 hours a week of TV viewing and see 400 TV
commercials in that time: it's a fast-moving mélange of Batman, Bulletman, Spiderman, Jeannie, Barbie, Ring Dings, Milk
Duds, Sugar Smacks, violent acts, Mork, Mindy, and money.
The average child spends more time looking at this material
than he does talking, playing, or reading. Kids of all ages
watch not only by day but also by night; 18 million children
are still in the viewing audience between 8 and 9 P.M., and no
fewer than 1 million are still watching at midnight! By the
time the child finishes high school, he will have spent 18,000
hours with the "TV curriculum" and only 12,000 with the
school curriculum.

Habitual viewing hasn't produced any conventional insight
into the significance of this behavior, nor have we made any
systematic inquiry into the cumulative effects of TV viewing
on the young. Meanwhile, people in all age groups tend to
watch more and more television each year—no matter what
the programs are! And now, a second explosion of TV
technology that is likely to increase viewing time dramatically
is upon us.

In the 1980's the proliferation of new video technologies

will transform current patterns in programming, distribution, and viewing as cable, two-way cable, pay cable, fiber optics, satellites, home-video recorders, and video disks hit the mass market. "Cable"—so named because it transmits signals via a coaxial cable rather than over the air—is now used in about 16 percent of U.S. households, and, by the end of the decade, 50 percent are expected to be using the system. Cable television threatens conventional broadcasting by making possible a vast number of channels in every home and potentially an almost infinite library of entertainment programs. This will pose formidable competition to the stations bound by advertising schedules which, say, run *The Flintstones* twice on the same day. New cable enterprises, such as Warner Communications' "Nickelodeon: The Young People's Satellite Network," promise all-day programming that aims to be nonviolent, noncommercial, nonsexist, and nonpropagandistic. Already in 1 million homes, this channel includes a mix of animation, vintage movies, films produced for schools, read-aloud comic-book presentations, music, and teen-age forums.

Home-video tape recording and playback devices are increasingly popular. Introduced in 1975, estimated sales grew to 30,000 in 1977 and 402,000 in 1978. The home recorder can tape off the air for future viewing while the viewer is asleep, away, or watching another channel. If the video recorder's growth parallels that of the TV set, within a decade most of us will own one. The attractions of TV will be virtually boundless.

So, as we are about to be "liberated" from the networks' schedules, we may be addicted more thoroughly and blindly than ever to the viewing habit. It is therefore now more imperative than ever that we understand the cumulative effects of television watching, particularly upon young children. Common sense tells us that we are all being affected, and none so decidedly as our children. In fact we now have evidence that habitual viewing can affect a young person's basic outlook and sensibilities, predisposition to violence and hyperactivity, IQ, reading ability, imagination, play, language patterns, critical thinking, self-image, perception of others, and values in general. Further, habitual TV viewing can affect the physical self as it can alter brain waves, reduce critical eye movements, immobilize the hands and body, and undermine nutrition and eating habits.

Twenty years ago a prominent British researcher, Dr. Hilde Himmelweit, reassured concerned parents by saying: "Television always enters a pattern of influences that already exist: the home, the peer group, the school, the church and the culture generally." In recent times Marie Winn disagreed. "But television does not merely influence the child," she writes in *The Plug-In Drug—Television and the Family*, "it deeply influences that *pattern of influences* that is meant to ameliorate its effects" (italics mine).

Winn is right. As the cumulative pattern of influences flows from television, we begin to see radical cultural effects; we see them in the United States, and I believe they will be seen increasingly in other parts of the world as the experience of television becomes more and more pervasive. Ritual and structure are disappearing from the home. When families use television routinely, the social structure and rituals of the group tend to be regulated by its viewing patterns. In all societies culture is transmitted to its children through rites, rules, rituals, and celebrations of its groups. A ritual can be thought of as a set of actions carried out in a ceremonial way, usually in a given time, at a given place; rituals have a binding quality and tie participants who share in them. They include traditional family activities such as having dinner together, sharing conversation, playing, celebrating holidays, bedtime conversation, games. But family interaction is declining. Large numbers of children report that they eat meals alone before the TV set, spend after-school hours watching TV instead of playing, and would rather "give up father" than give up TV. They say that they go to school "after *Huckleberry Hound*," eat a TV dinner "during *Gilligan's Island*," and go to bed "after *Charlie's Angels*." On Thanksgiving the preparation of the family feast will be timed to the football game and the media event will preempt the family event.

While these circumstances are not caused by television

alone, they are occurring in the same era when TV has completely penetrated the American family, capturing attention and time that were once available for group activity. It seems that as traditional institutions have crumbled (under pressure of divorce, mobility, absence of extended family), television has filled in the spaces. As a result, the transmission of culture to children does not come so much through the family as it comes from outside—mainly via television.

A major difference between the family and school of the past and those of today lies in their sources of information, entertainment, and learning. Before television, family members were more available to each other: wisdom came from elders close at hand and from the direct experiences of growing up. School was also a major source of information, and play was the child's entertainment. For these, the community offered context or structure. Inside this structure, parents raised children in the ways that they had learned from their own parents. Children developed their senses through play, discovering along the way how to use their hands, imaginations, and social skills while experiencing lots of human contact in learning. This life met many of the child's basic needs, and eventually most children learned to trust, to care, to think, to communicate, and to value what their elders valued. Through the rituals of family life, culture was handed down.

Now culture is handed up. Packaged in rock music, situation comedies, and TV advertisements, mass media delivers culture to the young who hand it up to adults. Since the 1950's and 1960's, American radio and TV have teased youth into new tastes and values and then played to these in large and profitable dimensions. Mass media were responsible for that time in the 1950's when the young began calling the tunes and the youth culture was born. Now, from the cities of the Soviet Union to the farmlands of Argentina, rock music, jeans, and "the Pepsi generation"—transported by media—are reorganizing not only our own families but families everywhere.

Coming to terms with the effects of television on children

will require vigorous and simultaneous efforts at home, in school, and in public forums. TV is the dominant cultural force in our society, yet no agency or institution has examined or dealt with its cumulative effects. At this moment, very few parents monitor or control the viewing behavior of their young; schools do little to acknowledge that television is an integral part of childhood; and the Federal Communications Commission (FCC), which theoretically regulates broadcasting, has been relatively "powerless" against TV because the networks are so secure and dominant with their enormous annual profits.

In several instances, government and private citizens' groups have tried to discover and report the effects of TV on children. They have been frustrated or suffocated by well-funded industry opposition. Two of the largest investigations, the Surgeon General's Report on TV and Social Behavior (1969–72) and the Action for Children's Television (ACT) probe (1968–present) had origins in humanitarian outrage at the fact that violence is used as entertainment on TV for the purpose of amassing large profits.

In the late 1960's, the Surgeon General was commissioned, with $8 million in Government funding, to determine whether there is a "causal relationship" between viewing TV violence and subsequent aggressive behavior. In 1972 the findings were reported in five official volumes titled *Television and Social Behavior—A Technical Report to the Surgeon General's Scientific Advisory Committee on Television and Social Behavior.* To produce this, twelve selected experts reviewed masses of researchers' data. In the concluding hearings, each of the twelve experts testified that he or she did find the evidence to show a causal relationship. From the beginning, however, industry pressure had been exerted to adjust and tone down the content of the report, first by "blackballing" prestigious researchers such as Albert Bandura from the committee, and later by insisting on compromises in the language of the summary of the report. No major change has occurred as a result of the $8-million report, even though it provided us (ten years ago) with a basis for action.

Other reports that might have contributed to our awareness have been suppressed, ignored, or swept under the rug, including those on dangerous levels of microwave radiation from TV sets and transmitters. Volumes of testimony on the health hazards involved in consuming the highly sugared junk foods that are heavily advertised on children's TV have in effect been ignored.

The most massive attempt to suppress information about the effects of TV is being carried on *now* as three powerful industries (broadcasting, advertising, manufacturing) have mobilized to fight consumer groups and the Federal Trade Commission (FTC) who are endeavoring to continue hearings on proposed regulation of TV advertising aimed at young children.

In a staff report, the FTC recommended that TV advertising to children be sharply curtailed because it exploits their immaturity in numerous ways. The concept, first formally advocated by Action for Children's Television, a national group based in Newtonville, Massachusetts, is now espoused by a number of organizations, including the American Academy of Pediatrics, the American Public Health Association, the Consumers' Union, the National Association of Elementary School Principals, and dozens more.

When the FTC slated hearings on the issue, the broadcasting, advertising, and manufacturing industries raised a *$30-million* war chest to launch a three-pronged attack on the proposed legislation. In a special report to its members, the Association of National Advertisers (ANA) said that a coalition had been formed to "neutralize" both press and FTC hearings; they proposed to work through the courts, through the Congressional appropriations process, and by influencing public opinion. Giant lobbies used the war chest to hire an army of attorneys and two of New York's largest public relations firms (Burson-Marsteller and Hill & Knowlton) to do battle against the consumer protection agencies.

At this writing the *Washington Star* headline reads: "Senate Panel Votes to Kill Regulation of Children's TV." The Senate Commerce Committee voted to adopt an amendment to the

FTC authorization bill, which would remove the "unfairness standard" from FTC consideration of advertising abuse. This would stop the rulemaking on children's advertising—the only rulemaking affected by the amendment. If the full Senate and House agree to the amendment, then the policy makers are in effect refusing to protect children through regulation. They are (in this case) denying parents and teachers vital information about the effects of TV which they need in order to manage TV at the consumers' end.

Meanwhile, ACT, the leading advocacy group in this matter, does its work from the second floor of an old frame house that is badly in need of a paint job. A staff of only ten people works week in and week out to get its message across. Peggy Charren, ACT president, points out that the combined salaries of her staff don't equal the salary of one top broadcasting executive. "Economically, it's a David and Goliath story," she says. "But there is no question that ACT will continue to focus on issues of children and television and work to make Government institutions responsive to citizen needs."

Television is troubling because we have no structures for managing it: at home where new perspectives could prevent TV from usurping childhood and injuring family relationships, at school where TV could be an object of inquiry and a carrier of ideas, and in the society at large where television must be harnessed to serve the public interest. Change will require broad awareness based on information; this will be a long-term battle, especially if the free flow of information is sabotaged by the television industry. We need to know much more about the effects of television on children, and until we do it is highly questionable whether we should permit such high levels of viewing by children during their most important developmental years.

▪ 2 ▪
THE
PHYSICAL
EFFECTS

Today's children are the first generation
exposed to over-stimulation, and we know nothing
of its long-term consequences.

Marianne Frankenhaeuser
University of Stockholm

While many speculations have been made on the effects of
television on human behavior, the effects of television viewing
on the human body itself have been virtually overlooked. Yet
proof piles up that habitual and cumulative TV viewing affects
people as biological organisms and probably produces a
number of significant adverse effects. What commentary there
has been has focused on the psychological cost of television
watching, but we should surely look at the physiological cost
to the child whose critical early development is so dependent
upon physical well-being and sensory input.

It is clear that the barrage of stimuli of modern society
produces real physical stress. This stress can be measured in
terms of changes in the electrical activity of the brain, in the
heart rate, in blood pressure, in the secretion of hormones, and
in a variety of consequent diseases. It is now possible to
observe, measure, and monitor the arousing and relaxing
influences of a given environment, and experts have identified

a widespread condition they call sensory overload. Sensory overload is damaging to all human beings, but especially to the young.

We know that if all the kitchen appliances are running and someone turns on the air conditioner, the system might become overloaded, fuses may blow, or the current may be cut off completely. In his book, *Overload*, psychiatrist Leopold Bellak explains that the brain, too, is a complex system of electric circuitry which, when overloaded with stimuli, can "short circuit." Such an overload condition is fed not only by the strain of living with the speed of modern technology, but also by the impact of crowding, rapid travel, and any general confusion at home or school. "What has us spinning," says Bellak, "is the tremendous overloading of our senses. We are hit with *too much, too fast.* Our signals are conflicting; what is worse, there are too many of them, and they are constantly changing."

When rhesus monkeys at the University of Miami Medical School were subjected to the sounds of alarm clocks, radios, traffic, telephones, and television for three weeks, the monkeys' average blood pressure increased by 43 percent. Exactly which part of a person's (or monkey's) overload can be attributed to television is hard to say. However, we do know that in most households the TV is turned on at breakfast time and plays almost constantly throughout the day and evening—through housework, homework, naptimes, mealtimes, telephone calls, and personal conversations. Whether the people at home watch it, or listen to it, or simply coexist with the turned-on TV, its sounds and flickers must be taken into account as a major stimulus—like electronic wallpaper—that is acting upon people more continuously than any other.

It is worth investigating whether *anybody* should spend so many hours with TV. But in the case of children who are growing up on continuous television there is special concern. We know the power of the stimulus, and we are especially aware of the vulnerability of the very young nervous system. Nobody yet understands how cumulative television viewing will affect the development of the human species in the long run, but evidence is emerging to show how TV viewing affects such individual physical responses as brain waves, eye movements, the use of the hands, and overall body movements. It is vital for us to know more and to understand how our bodies respond to television and how respective physical responses relate to each other.

BRAIN WAVES

The brain, like the heart and all muscles, is alive with electrical activity. This activity of the cells can be measured in volts, recorded, and charted in ways that help to explain what is going on inside the body.

Using ordinary radio equipment, neurologist Hans Berger in 1924 amplified the brain's electrical impulses more than a million times and translated the rhythms of the brain cells onto paper so that they could be studied. This invention which could "take the pulse" of the brain became the electroencephalograph, or EEG. With this tool, scientists can tell which part of the brain is working and which is not; it can show when the mind is relaxed and when it is actively concentrating.

The most common type of brain waves—those which can be recorded during most of a person's waking hours—are the medium-paced "Beta" waves, which are typically associated with "alert" activities such as focusing, paying attention, reading, talking, cooking dinner, driving a car, playing ball, etc. A marked slowdown of electrical activity in the brain will be measured and charted on the EEG as long, slow alpha waves; these are associated with lack of eye movement, fixation, lack of definition, idleness, inactivity, and overall body inertness. Alpha waves occur when the individual is "not orienting." But, when the person orients to something, "gives visual commands," or notices anything outside himself, then he produces immediate increase in faster wave activity and the alpha state disappears.

Dr. Erik Peper, a professor at San Francisco State University and a researcher on electroencephalographic testing, says, "Alpha occurs when you don't orient to. You can sit back and have pictures in your head, but you are in a totally passive condition and unaware of the world outside of your pictures . . . the right phrase for alpha is really 'spaced out.'"

Highly altered brain-wave states tend to be produced when people watch TV for more than a few minutes.[1] Most people's EEGs show alpha waves—or sleep patterns—after only 20 minutes of TV viewing. A smaller percentage, however, are excited to a state of hyperactivity or even epileptic fits which are charted by the EEG as rapid "spiked" waves. In either case, the individual is not employing "critical viewing skills," and it is safe to say that TV has the upper hand—if not control—at this point. Why is it that when an individual is exposed to TV his brain waves might either race frantically or show sleep patterns? What is the role of individual differences? What is the role of television viewing in this phenomenon?

"SPACED-OUT" VIEWER IDENTIFIED

Jerry Mander is one writer who has tied together what solid scientific research exists on how brain waves and memory might be affected by the experience of television viewing. He began his probe by visiting the Brain Information Service of the Bio-Medical Library of UCLA, where he asked for a computer scan of any materials that could relate TV viewing to physiological syndromes, including hypnosis, addiction, hyperactivity, and the neurophysiology of light reception. He had become interested in these subjects after noticing how often people of all ages comment about the addictive or mesmerizing nature of TV viewing: "I feel hypnotized, brainwashed, like a vegetable, drugged, spaced out, it's turning my mind to mush, my kids look like zombies." Two thousand anecdotal reports suggested that often the people who described themselves as "spaced out" actually liked the experience because it helped them to forget about their otherwise overloaded, hassled lives. A literary critic described the kid on a television high as "equipped with thumb and blanket—the glazed eye, the noncommunicative state, the total stupor that can't be broken into. . . ."

Dr. Gerald Lesser, a psychologist at Harvard and one of the chief advisors to Children's Television Workshop in New York, described this behavior: "Some children can view television for hours with their eyes rarely leaving the set. We were so struck by this viewing style when we first began doing research that we coined the term 'zombie viewer' to refer to the child that sat seemingly hypnotized in front of the set." He noted that other children constantly keep a check on all outside activities in the room while they view; the style of viewing, however, was no guarantee of how much the child was absorbing from the program.

Each of these observers is describing the experience of slow brain waves, or alpha waves, which represent one of the responses to watching the flickering light of a TV screen. One scientific study of brain waves and TV, by psychologists Merrelyn and Fred Emery at the Australian National University at Canberra, shows that in viewing any television, human brain wave activity enters a characteristic pattern; in other words, the response is to the medium itself rather than to any of its content. They say that once the set goes on, the brain waves slow down until the preponderance of alpha and related waves become the habitual pattern. The longer the set is on, the slower the waves become. Precisely which program is being viewed makes no difference in the development of this pattern.

In a landmark study with ten children, Dr. Thomas Mulholland, a colleague of Peper, found that even when watching their "favorite" show, the children's brain waves did not respond to the content but to the act of watching. Brain waves, apparently, do not distinguish between "boring" or "exciting" content, "good" or "bad" shows. When Mulholland asked the children to be interested and involved in the programming, he looked for an oscillation between alpha slow-wave and beta—but that didn't happen. The kids just sat and watched and remained in alpha most of the time. Peper, who worked on the project with Mulholland, noted:

> This meant that while they were watching they were not reacting, not orienting, not focusing . . . just spaced out. The horror of television is that the information goes in, but we don't react to it. It goes right into our memory pool and perhaps we react to it later, but we don't know what we're reacting to. When you watch television you are training yourself not to react and so later on, you're doing things without knowing why you're doing them or where they came from.

Meditation is commonly associated with the alpha state—yet that activity is in clear contrast to the "zombie viewer." The important difference between the two is that in meditation you are producing your own material (ideas), but in TV viewing the ideas and images are not internally generated but come from outside. Television does not arouse active attention; rather, TV viewing suppresses it. According to psychologist-hypnotist Dr. Freda Morris, people who are good at meditation are difficult to hypnotize. They start going into hypnotic trance, but at a certain point they begin producing their own material and cannot be influenced by outside instruction unless they want to be. "Television addiction might itself be symptomatic of an inability to produce one's own mental imagery," she says.

The alpha state, when it is associated with TV viewing, seems to be a response to the experience of watching a TV screen rather than to specific pictures or programs. ("The medium is the message," as Marshall McLuhan said.) What element of the medium might account for these effects on brain waves? Some researchers believe that it is *light*—the particular kind of artificial light delivered by television.

It has been known for a long time that certain kinds of light and sound can be stressful to the brain and nervous system. Important clues are offered in certain medical cases. For example, the intense glare on a sunny beach has frequently produced seizures in epileptics. Other kinds of photo stimulation—such as light flickering through the leaves of trees—has produced "absences" or temporary amnesia in some people.

Television is an intense kaleidoscope of moving light and sound. It can create extreme excitement in the brain and, after prolonged viewing, it can produce a "drugged state" and alpha waves in the brain. Dr. T. Berry Brazelton, a pediatrician who teaches at Harvard University, hypothesized that the flickering lights of television *simultaneously* stir up the child and make the child passive. Brazelton conducted an experiment with infants that demonstrates the power of bright lights to both excite the child's nervous system and to numb it at the same time. He exposed a group of peacefully resting babies to bright operating-room lights that were flashed on for three seconds and off for one. In this pattern the flashes were repeated 20 times while the babies' responses (including heartbeat and brain waves) were recorded. The first time the light was turned on, the babies were startled and noticeable changes occurred in their heartbeat and respiration. After a few flashes, the intensity of their reaction tapered off. By the fifteenth flash, sleep patterns appeared on the brain chart (EEG) although it was clear that the babies' eyes were still taking in light.

Brazelton explains:

> Our experiments demonstrated that the newborn has a marvelous shutdown device for dealing with disturbing stimuli: he can tune them out and go into a sleeplike state. But if we can imagine the amount of energy a newborn baby expends in managing this kind of shutdown—energy he could put to better use—we can see how expensive this mechanism becomes.

Dr. Brazelton proposes:

> Just like the operating room light, television creates an environment that assaults and overwhelms the child; he can respond to it only by bringing into play his shutdown mechanism, and thus become more passive. I have observed this in my own children, and I have seen it in other

people's children. As they sat in front of a television that was blasting away, watching a film of horrors of varying kinds, the children were completely quiet. . . . They were hooked.[2]

Each human being, according to inborn sensitivities, will respond differently to a potent stimulus. Through practice or familiarity a person may become "habituated" or accustomed to a particular influence such as light, dark, noise, etc. But when habituation doesn't easily occur, another response may be employed to defend or protect the organism. The "turn-off" response, described by Brazelton, Emery, and Mulholland, is one kind of response to an extreme environment.

However, some people with certain vulnerabilities do not "turn off" but "turn on" in response to the extreme environment of flickering light. According to reports in the prestigious British medical journal *Lancet*, increasing numbers of people have experienced fits or seizures while viewing television. In one study, the journal reports, "Many of these patients (98 of 176) experience absences or seizures *only* while viewing television and usually when they are close to the set, adjusting the picture or switching channels. At least half of these patients have normal EEGs except when they are exposed to photic stimulation."[3] The physicians have labeled this response "television epilepsy."

Another article, entitled "Self-Induced Television Epilepsy," in the *Canadian Psychiatric Association Journal*, describes a twelve-year-old who fixes her gaze on the TV screen, moves within 3 to 6 inches of it, then changes channels rapidly or lets the image roll horizontally. As her vision blurs, she feels "jerks" inside her body as she develops a generalized epileptic seizure. "I go to the set to focus it and I can't pull myself away, it's like a magnetic attraction. I can't say what's happening," she said.[4]

While "television epilepsy" is an unusual response to TV, hyperactivity is a common response among children. When school psychologists and teachers speak of the "TV Syndrome," they are referring to the child who seems too tired to pay attention for more than a couple of seconds yet is too restless or hyperactive to sit still or control his or her aggressive behavior. Hyperactivity is increasing rapidly as a recognized malady in America's nursery and elementary schools. According to a report by Dr. Werner I. Halpern, the psychiatrist who heads the Rochester (N.Y.) Mental Health Clinic, in the early 1970's there has been a sudden increase in two-year-olds who were referred to the clinic for behavior disturbances. They were restless, hyperactive, and frantic. Their speech was inappropriate and they compulsively recited serial numbers and letters learned from Sesame Street. He said that usually these recitations occurred in the absence of any apparent cues. "They often inspected their inanimate surroundings like restless, wound-up robots. But none of these children was psychotic, autistic, schizophrenic or retarded." [5]

Halpern's clinic team observed that the children who were brought to the clinic were all regular viewers of Sesame Street and suggested this restlessness might be more widespread than the first cases might convey. Says Halpern:

> Of course, many parents rationalize their children's productions as evidence of alertness or even superior intelligence, although they credit Sesame Street as the catalytic agent. Only when associated symptoms appear which are distressing to parents, such as uncontrolled overactivity, prolonged sleep resistance, or intractable irritability, do parents seek professional help.

When the parents of Halpern's young patients cut out the viewing of Sesame Street, these children improved dramatically. He contends that the rapidity and choppiness of the Sesame Street images prevent reflection and the adaptive capacity of children from entering into the learning process. Overloading of the sensory receptors creates a feeling of powerlessness. While these effects are true for all children, innate characteristics in certain children create higher susceptibility to the consequent tension and overload. Halpern concludes:

The jived-up repetitive auditory and visual experience
evidently may be too much for some children to assimilate or avoid successfully. When their nervous systems
become overtaxed, they resort to diffuse tension discharge
behaviors, exemplified by unfocused hyperactivity and
irritability. In animal research, at least, younger creatures
are more susceptible to the diminution of adaptive capacities in the face of stress and to the induction of neuroses
than are older ones. A similar condition for children
points to the possibility that sensory overload may pre-
cipitate more than transient behavior problems.

However, Dr. Edward Palmer, vice-president for research at
Children's Television Workshop (CTW), the production
agency for *Sesame Street*, objects to Halpern's attacking
Sesame Street for effects that may be stimulated by television
in general. He says, "There is not one shred of scientific
research which supports Halpern in naming *Sesame* as the
cause of the behavior he observed."

Others have reasoned that TV viewing causes or exacerbates
hyperactivity by projecting images into the brain of the viewer
who is *sitting still*. While seeing the images stimulates the
impulse to move, responding to a machine is ludicrous;
therefore, stimulation is repressed. Mander calls this effect a
"sensory tease."

The physical energy which is created by the images, but
not used, is physically stored. Then when the set is off, it
comes bursting outward in aimless, random, speedy activity. I have seen it over and over again with children.
They are quiet while watching. Then afterwards they
become overactive, irritable and frustrated.

Countless parents have reported the same "withdrawal" symptoms in their children. The Emerys go so far as to predict that
as television advances in Australia there will be a directly
proportional increase in hyperactivity. Whether TV children
respond with hyperactivity or by spacing out, what is going on

ir brains is closely related to what is going on with their
~~eyes.~~

EYE MOVEMENTS

One accepted estimate is that 80 percent of what is learned is
gained through the eyes. The way a person learns is pro-
foundly affected by the images that come to the brain via the
eyes. People gather visual information in many ways—looking
around, reading, watching TV.

Reading proficiency is a vital cultural skill. It means more
than recognizing road signs and product labels. To function
easily in school and the society at large, a person must read
well. Despite the 144 million TV sets in the United States, all
of our major institutions are print-based—that is, they depend
on print material and people using print in order to function.
In addition, studies show that a youngster's self-esteem and
self-image are linked to his ability to read; it is still the
expectation in this culture. Yet in the United States there is a
serious literacy slump.

Loss of eye movement is one significant cause of the drop in
literacy. Correcting eye movement deficiencies will not produce instant literacy, but parents and educators who are trying
to develop reading abilities in children should be aware of the
necessary motor aspect of good vision. Children cannot read
well if they cannot see well. To see, the eyes must respond to
light, focus, and transmit images to the brain. But the eyes
must do much more *in order to read*. Reading requires a
physical technique in which the eyes *must move*. Most
children spend less time with books than they do with TV.
And, while it is often recognized that eye movements are
necessary in order to read, what is not generally realized is
that television trains eyes *not* to move. Scientific studies have
demonstrated that eyes move less while watching TV than in
almost any other activity in daily living.

Much of what is known about learning to read has been
discovered through studies of the eyes and eye movements.

When reading, the eyes start out at the beginning of a paragraph, stay there an instant, move part of the way across the line, stop briefly, move again, and so on until the end of the line is reached. Then the eyes make a return sweep to the beginning of the next line and continue to move and pause, move and pause, across the page. Words are grasped only during the pauses, but the smooth and efficient system of scanning the line is basic to the reading process. Good readers make fewer stops per line and take in more words during each pause than poor readers.

The fact that there are differences between the eye movements of good as against poor readers suggests the possibility that reading may be improved by training the poor reader to imitate the eye movements of the good reader. Numerous therapies and speed-reading courses have been developed in an effort to do this.

One vision expert, Dr. Edgar Gording, of the Gording Clinic for Developmental Vision, says:

> When we see a child who can't read, we first check out how his eyes are moving—older kids who aren't reading often have faulty eye movements. Vision, he explains, is one of the five senses, but it is also a physical skill. He points out that there is only one cranial nerve for the sensory act of vision but there are three nerves that enable the eyes to move right, left, up, down, in and out in a synchronized way. In order to read, it is necessary to execute these movements precisely and to see single—not double—when viewing at close range. This achievement is called binocular vision. The prerequisites for reading call for single simultaneous binocular vision. If the eyes do not move properly and if they are not able to aim the visual axes at the object, such as letters in a word, then the child trying to read will see double. The closer we bring material to the eyes the more exact the eye movements have to be because the eyes have to traverse a greater angle. Television watching calls for little or no eye movement because of the small angle crossed over by the

screen at the distance generally watched. Furthermore, the
pull of the television screen tends to keep the eyes looking
in one direction, causing the further loss of eye movement.[6]

In therapy sessions at his clinic, Dr. Gording stimulates eye
movement in children and adults.

> About 30–40 percent of the kids referred to me have been
> previously labeled "retarded." Usually they aren't re-
> tarded, they just can't do certain things, like read. Most of
> them will exhibit little or no eye movement. The first
> thing we do is get those eyes moving!

Gording claims that most of these children improve their
reading so much through his developmental-vision therapy
that they are not considered retarded when they complete the
treatment.

Others can benefit from eye movement retraining. The world
champion Pittsburgh Pirates contracted with Gording to put
the entire team through "developmental vision," believing
that it would improve their abilities to hit home runs and shag
fly balls. Gording's program, which teaches the eyes to zero in
on an object, became an integral part of the Pirates' spring
training in 1979. "Our people learn not only hand and eye
coordination, but foot and eye coordination. We have a new
line of exercises, based on the idea that the whole body is
involved in seeing. . . . Our people train on their feet. They do
not sit down. We involve the whole body."

Branch B. Rickey, assistant director of minor leagues, witnessed Gording's program and concluded that "the demand on
eyesight is greater in baseball than almost all other sports."
Another team manager said, "Certainly a man who can see
better, concentrate better and perform better visual skills will
also physically accomplish more. It will give an athlete
another tool to increase his innate abilities."

If, like other motor skills, eye movements can be taught
through practice, shouldn't we be examining the kind of

practice most children get during the period of early growth and development—and throughout the years when they are being taught to read? Yet, this is precisely the time in childhood when most children spend many hours a day in front of the TV, practicing the very eye movements (i.e., none) that later take great effort to unlearn.

It is of course important not to oversimplify ideas about learning to read and remedying reading problems. An incredulous reading teacher asked Gording at a lecture, "Do you mean that *you* teach children to move their eyes, so that *we* can teach them to read?"

"That's right!" he answered. But, in addition, he said there are things that could be done to change the impact of TV on eye movements:

1. Not all shows should be in color, because of the increased "pull" of the color screen.
2. Classrooms should have large screens, if any, because large pictures encourage eye movement.
3. TV should not be the babysitter. No child under four ought to be placed in front of the set.[7]

Gording's proposals are sound according to what we know about vision and growth. If, as he says, "human beings must obey their visual commands," those commands can be adjusted by adjusting the environment, including the flow of TV stimuli.

USE OF THE HANDS AND BODY

Experiments and therapies of various kinds indicate that using the hands and body during early childhood promotes the child's entire perceptual development. Reports from kindergarten teachers across the land strongly suggest that kids can't *do* many of the things they *used to do* with their hands, and there is evidence of a decline in small-muscle development. The far-reaching effects of immobilized hands logically extends to visual and mental operations. Throughout centuries of human development the functions of the hands, eyes, and brain have been intertwined. Motor input to the brain is almost as important as visual input; one complements the other.

Today's children enter kindergarten after being conditioned by thousands of hours of television watching. As a result, they increasingly arrive in school with a deficit in their physical experience. One critical deficit is in the use of the hands—an experience that formerly came to children as an inevitable part of play and growing up. No longer, because kids today spend more time *sitting* watching TV than in any other waking activity. *Sitting* itself has been implicated in problems of the spine, nerves, back, and neck, as well as in the immobility of the eyes and hands which is promoted by TV viewing. Studies also show that while children are sitting and watching they are not usually engaged in any other activity or "parallel play"— they are just passively watching. In one typical study 193 elementary school students were asked, "What do you do while you are watching TV?" Sixty-one percent—a clear majority—replied, "Nothing." Those who reported doing "something" most frequently named *eating* as the activity. Other occasionally reported activities included "fooling around, lying on Mother's bed, falling asleep, petting the dog, punching my brother."

Today's kindergarten teachers report with alarm a significant decline in the manual abilities of five-year-olds. For example, an experienced British teacher now teaching in the United States says:

> It used to be that I could expect five- and six-year-olds to use a pair of scissors. We do a lot of cutting and pasting and building with scrap at this level. Now, many children don't know how to begin a cutting activity. They'll stick their first two fingers through the holes and the scissors will just hang down. I can teach them, of course, but only after a lot more basic work with the hands. I will drop back a few notches on the developmental scale—teach them to *tear* the paper (hundreds of times) and to paste, string beads and build things—and later reintroduce the scissors. The point is, kids used to get this experience at

home. There's a general difference in what you can expect now compared with 10 or 15 years ago. And, of course, those who do the least seem to be those who watch TV the most.

Scores of teachers give similar reports. Vision experts believe that vision-directed movements by the hands and body promote the binocular vision so necessary for reading. Hence therapists have a roster of exercises that involve the whole body—especially eye–hand and eye–foot coordination. These exercises are employed to improve the *functioning of the eyes,* the major "supplier" of sensory data to the brain.

So related are hand–eye–brain functions that anthropologists believe that when humans began to use *hands* to make *tools* (some 4 million years ago), this activity promoted the growth of the brain to its unprecedented human size. The widely held belief is that in the long course of human evolution erect posture freed the hands to make tools, and, with this capacity, the enlarged brain developed. In a sense, the theory goes, intensified handwork produced expanded brain work.

The theory prompts fascinating questions. If the eyes, hands, and brain work together as a team, and if accelerating the workings of the hands means accelerating the workings of the brain, what would happen if one of those members is immobilized or impaired? If increased handwork was responsible for stimulating the development of the larger brain, might not diminished handwork eventually cause a diminished brain? If some "magical force" were to enter our cultural environment and "capture" or "tie up" the hands, wouldn't this in some way affect the course of brain development? Whatever the answer, it appears that TV viewing tends to immobilize the hands of the young during their key developmental stage.

Numerous studies by social scientists point up the importance of motor input to sensory/brain development. In one laboratory experiment researchers restrained one kitten from moving its limbs while letting a companion kitten move freely. The kittens were rigged to an apparatus that required that one kitten ride in a gondola all day (with its paws never touching the ground) while the other kitten pushed the gondola in a circular pattern. At the end of a ten-day experiment, the kitten that had done the walking showed normal perception; it blinked at approaching objects and put up its paws to avoid collisions. The kitten who rode the gondola did not make perceptual responses. It had become perceptually retarded.

This experiment illustrates the principle cited earlier that sensory input without the complementary involvement of the muscles can be meaningless to the organism. Without motor commitment, learning can be drastically reduced.

The principle is demonstrated again by the baby with a mobile dangling over its crib. The mobile will catch the attention of the child for a while, but if he can't touch it or cause it to move, he will lose interest. However, in one experiment, where a string was tied to the toe of a three-week-old baby and also tied to the mobile, the child quickly discovered how to move the mobile by moving his foot. He could himself exercise control and therefore remained interested.

Similarly, teachers and other experts use physical activities to correct lagging language development, poor self-image, and lack of awareness of the space close at hand. Experts will even plan extra hand and body exercises when the child shows learning delays. The four-year-old is helped by putting pegs in holes, stringing beads, making things, taking things apart; all of these promote cognitive development as well as small muscle agility. One teacher of "normal four-year-olds with language delays" says: "I want the kids involved in *real*, direct activities—not books and symbols or even such abstract material as puzzles. Three- and four-year-olds should not have reading and paper–pencil activities pushed at them these days at the expense of more appropriate physical activities."

Television intervenes in the eye–hand–brain marriage, and the intervention typically now starts shortly after birth. Consider how babies normally see and move and learn. The infant begins to learn vision by fixating on his own wiggling hand waving in front of him. When his hand waves to the left, his

eyes move to the left, and then to the right, and so on. This is
the beginning of vision-directed movement of the body and
eye movements of the type associated with reading, as well as
eye–hand coordination of the type required to bat a ball or clap
hands.

Yet researchers in laboratory settings have found that babies'
eyes are most easily attracted by shifting patterns of reds,
greens, and blues. If sound is added to the color stimulus, the
combination becomes an especially powerful attraction, also
capable of sustaining infants' attention. Isn't this what a color
TV set is—a changing pattern rich in the colors that infants
find most attractive? What's more, it combines changing visual
patterns with sound. So the infant's eyes—and the hands
which he formerly watched and played with—are distracted
from their normal activities by this "magical" force. Mothers
often nurse their babies in front of the TV. Rather than watch
the mother's face—as babies have always done before—these
infants will watch the TV. The child will very early become a
habitual viewer by obeying the visual commands of the TV
stimulus.

Toddlers who sit motionless watching TV—even in the
presence of many toys and nearby family activity—are highly
inclined to passivity. If the child's eyes had not been so
powerfully drawn to TV, his hands and body would be more
actively engaged in normal preschool activities. There would
be more time and inclination to fit shapes together, line up
blocks, build, tie, button, sort, stack, pour, put together, take
apart—in a word, to manipulate and coordinate mind and
hands. Later they would cut, paste, tear, draw, dig, sew. In all
of these acts, hands are used and the small muscles are
developed—along with the eyes and brains.

But children who watch a lot of television do not do as much
of this—and the consequences are beginning to show up.

Ironically, the sensory-motor activities that the TV generation especially needs are precisely the activities that are being
dropped from school life. These activities would have occurred routinely in many "old-fashioned" art and gym programs. Erroniously, today, when citizens are cutting school

budgets, art and physical education are the first to go in the name of efficiency and responsibility.

MICROWAVE RADIATION FROM TV

In the 1960's a major report prepared by an independent researcher for the Raytheon Corporation concluded that if low-level microwave radiation proved to be biologically harmful there would be far greater hazard to the general population from television than from microwave ovens. Microwave radiation *can* be dangerous—and TV sets, particularly color sets, are one source of it. The Raytheon report, and others, have largely been covered up or swept under the rug, and as a result consumers are not really aware of the potential effects of low-level microwave radiation.

Microwaves are low-frequency radiowaves that can pass through or penetrate deeply into human tissues. Their cumulative effect has been associated with the development of numerous health problems. Paul Brodeur, author of *The Zapping of America,* says:

> Nature has not prepared us for this invisible assault. Radar technicians and electronics workers exposed to microwaves are developing cataracts, blood disorders, and cardiovascular problems. . . . Microwaves may cause human genetic damage. They may alter behavior, causing dizziness, headaches, irritability, loss of judgment and other disorders of the central nervous system.

Brodeur explains that these waves are beamed indiscriminately into the environment from television, radio, and radar transmitters; from telephone relay systems, orbiting satellites, and high-voltage power lines; from microwave ovens, diathermy machines, citizen band radios; and from a "vast arsenal" of military weapons and devices.[8]

In the mid-1960's, 400,000 color TV sets were recalled when it was discovered that component failure caused an unusual amount of radiation to be emitted. The Food and Drug

Administration (FDA) advised that people sit 6 feet away from their color sets or stop watching TV altogether.

Is the concern over low-level TV radiation warranted? The question is rarely raised. Some scientists who have noted the physical effects of TV that are described in this chapter— particularly the tendency toward both hyperactivity and leth- argy—believe that microwave radiation may be the cause. Dr. John Ott, director of the Environmental Health and Light Research Institute, in Sarasota, has written his version of the TV radiation story in his book, *Health and Light*.[9] Dr. Ott's attention was attracted by a November 6, 1964, report in *Time* magazine which described the presentation of two Air Force physicians at the American Academy of Pediatrics that year. They had studied 30 children whose symptoms included nervousness, continuous fatigue, headaches, loss of sleep, and vomiting. After all of the usual tests on food and water, and for infectious and childhood diseases, no explanation could be found. When it was discovered that all of these children were watching television three to six hours a day, and six to ten hours on Saturdays and Sundays, the doctors prescribed total abstinence from TV.

In the 12 families that enforced the rule, the children's symptoms vanished in two or three weeks; other parents reduced TV time to two hours a day, and the children's symptoms did not abate for five or six weeks. When viewing levels rose, the symptoms reappeared.

Many explanations for these physical effects were offered, but Ott was concerned that no consideration had been given to the possibility of radiation exposure. He was curious to find out if there might be a basic physiological response in plants or animals to "some sort of radiation or other form of energy" emanating from TV sets. In his greenhouse he set up an experiment using a large color TV set. One half of the picture tube was covered with a lead shield (the type used to block X rays) and the other half with black photographic paper that would allow radiation to penetrate. Six pots, each containing three bean seeds, were placed directly in front of the shielded half of the screen; an identical set of bean pots was placed in front of the unshielded half of the screen. Still another set of pots and beans was placed 50 feet outside of the greenhouse.

Ott reports that at the end of three weeks the beans outdoors and the pots in front of the lead shield showed 6 inches of apparently normal growth. But the beans in the pots that were exposed to the TV's microwave radiation showed "excessive vine-type growth" ranging up to 31½ inches, the leaves on the latter being about three times the size of the others.

These results caused Ott to set up a similar experiment with white rats. Two rats were each placed in separate cages in front of a color TV tube that was turned on six hours a day on weekdays and for ten hours on Saturdays and Sundays. One half was shielded and the other was not, as in the case of the beans. Ott reported: "The rats protected only with black paper became increasingly hyperactive and aggressive within three to ten days, and then became progressively lethargic. At 30 days they were extremely lethargic and it was necessary to push them to make them move about the cage." The rats shielded with the lead showed some similar abnormal be-havioral patterns, but to a considerably lesser degree and more time was required before these abnormal behavioral patterns became apparent, says Ott in *Health and Light*.

Ott's experiments and others like them will have to be repeated and elaborated before hard conclusions can be drawn. But Ott's findings to date already indicate serious cause for wide concern.

After the scare of the 1960's, the subject of TV radiation faded from the public consciousness. In 1968 Congress passed a law charging the Food and Drug Administration (FDA) with the responsibility for setting and enforcing standards for TV set radiation. New standards went into effect in 1970. It is now supposed to be the responsibility of the manufacturers to test their own sets and assure the FDA through written reports that the standards are being met.

If we assume that all sets are safe when they leave the factory, how do we know they are still safe a few months later when they are set up in the living room? Or six years later when they are still in use? Manufacturers do test the sets under conditions of stress, and according to an FDA spokesperson, components are designed to last for "the useful life of the set." But obviously sets can malfunction.

If the voltage level for a TV set is higher than it should be, excess radiation leakage can occur despite the precautions taken by the manufacturer. Voltage level can be raised—knowingly or unknowingly—by someone trying to fix a set, or the voltage control component can fail because of damage or deterioration. Then excess radiation leakage can occur, and there is no way for the average set owner to know. There is no reason for him even to suspect leakage, since no one has made him aware of the potential hazard in his living room.

The FDA publishes a pamphlet entitled, "We Want You to Know About Television Radiation." It recommends that set repairs be done by a qualified service person and that TV be watched "at a distance at which the image quality is satisfactory to the viewer." Whatever the FDA has in mind here, it is probably not the distance and quality most three-year-olds are willing to settle for.

Sets can be checked for radiation, but most people do not look into the problem because they do not know there is a problem. Should sets have periodic "checkups" for leakage? Is excess leakage a common problem? Does it occur only in color TV sets? How can people protect themselves against a danger that is both uncertain and invisible?

There are many unanswered questions surrounding this potential health hazard. No one knows for sure the cumulative effects of low-level radiation exposure. And no one knows for sure how many of the 73 million color sets in the United States are at this moment emitting excess radiation. Maybe it's time we started getting some answers.

Meanwhile, in most households at least one set is turned on for more than six hours a day. Children take TV for granted and often touch it and watch it at close range for many hours on end. New programs lure them closer. One, designed to elicit viewers' participation, even invites children to put their hands on the TV screen. In one episode of *Vice Versa* a prince wouldn't stop crying until someone could be found whose hand fit a magic glove. "Surely one of you out there must fit the glove," pleaded the TV character—as preschoolers rushed forward to "fit" their hands on the life-sized glove image on the screen.

The problem is not a malevolent TV producer but an uneducated public. Perhaps, as a first step, the FDA should require all TV sets manufactured to carry a warning (like microwave ovens) that says, "Beware—this set may be hazardous to your health." For now the FDA dispenses caution only through its pamphlet, which very few people have seen and which merely says, "To assure that a new television receiver is as X ray-free as is technically feasible, purchasers should check the back of the set for a label or tag certifying that it meets the Federal standard on emissions."

CAN WE ADAPT?

An older friend reminds: "I remember when the steam locomotive first came along . . . and physicians everywhere were cautioning people that the human body couldn't adapt to high-speed travel of 60 miles per hour. They predicted a soaring rate of coronaries." We did, of course, adapt to train travel—and to other changes—and we have come to assume that humans' adaptive capacity will always keep pace with change. Now, however, certain facts suggest that this may not be possible. Widespread stress and overload clearly suggest that there are limits to adaptability. Failing to respect the fragility of life, increasingly we are "blowing fuses."

We now have evidence that habitual television viewing produces major physical effects on our bodies. It can alter our brain waves, paralyze eye movements, immobilize the hands, irritate the central nervous system, assault the senses, impact us with microwave radiation, and even induce epileptic fits.

Certainly the evidence should be investigated thoroughly before we permit the family to sit in front of the TV set for many hours each week. This is especially true of young children because they are most vulnerable, and because damage done early in childhood is often irreversible.

What we know—for sure—is that children have a basic need for physical activity, appropriate mental stimulation, and sensory experience. The brilliant educator Maria Montessori wrote of the relationship of body and mind, environment and perception:

> These impressions not only penetrate
> the mind of the child
> but they form it.
> They become incarnated, for
> the child makes his own mental flesh
> in using the things that
> are in his environment.
> We have called this type of mind
> the absorbent mind and
> it is difficult for us to conceive
> the magnitude of its powers.

• 3 •

THE
EFFECTS
ON
LEARNING
AND
PERCEPTION

Is TV a Pied Piper? Yes, it is.
We had better be sure we know
where it is leading our children.

Dr. Dorothy H. Cohen
Bank Street College of Education

The young child has an "absorbent mind," said Maria Montessori. Children "soak up" the environment through their senses—by touching, seeing, smelling, hearing, tasting. In short, kids learn by doing.

Perception is not merely the absorbing or collecting of impressions but is the processing of all this "information" by the mind and body—the system by which the person makes meaning. Just as food that is swallowed must be metabolized in order to be used by the body, sights and sounds must be processed in order to be used by the mind. To perceive the world is to metabolize the sensory information that is received. A camera does not perceive, nor does a microphone. But a human being does.

Many factors affect the perceptual process, including the normal functioning of the senses, the brain, past experiences, intelligence, imagination, the nature of incoming messages, and the ability to pay attention.

Obviously, children can gain information from TV; they learn to sing commercials before they can talk and recite the ABC's before the symbols have meaning for them. Further, we have seen that the amazing medium that can teach cognitive skills, such as the recognition of numbers and letters, can also teach behaviors: how to dance a pirouette, how to hit a slice serve, how to execute a karate kick, how to use a hand gun, and how to want products. Television gives children stunningly complex pieces of information, but this knowledge is largely unintegrated and lacks sufficient context and meaning.

With understandable alarm, parents, physicians, and teachers are observing rising numbers of today's children who can't process information as well as they were once expected to do. They say that kids generally can't see, hear, or pay attention as well as most children did only ten years ago.

Experienced teachers, those who have taught long enough to know several generations of children, are coming to alarming conclusions about current learning styles and abilities: Kids can't listen for any length of time; they can't follow verbal directions very well; they can't pay attention ("When I read them stories out loud, they squirm and say, 'I can't hear it without pictures'"); children today can't wait or delay gratification; they can't process language as well as past generations; they don't seem motivated to use their imaginations.

Increasingly we must consider the possible role of television in producing these new and typical characteristics in children. For example, a relationship has already been established between heavy television viewing and low IQ scores. Michael Morgan and Larry Gross of the Annenberg School of Communications at the University of Pennsylvania compared the viewing habits of a group of sixth-to-ninth graders with their IQ scores and their level of academic achievement.[1] Students who were heavy viewers (i.e., who watched more than six hours a day) were more likely to have low IQ's than those who were light viewers (two hours or less a day). In their study, the amount of viewing time was a better predictor of IQ than any other variable tested, including social class. Academic achievement was also found to be related to viewing habits. Reading comprehension, in particular, is associated with TV viewing, and the association is generally a negative one. For most children, greater viewing and lower reading comprehension go hand in hand. The exception is heavy viewers with low IQ; their reading comprehension is actually slightly higher than that of light viewers on the same IQ level. Morgan and Gross's study does not claim to prove that heavy viewing creates poor readers. No one can say for sure if this is the case, or if poor readers seek satisfaction or entertainment in TV, or if the variables relate in still another way. But they are related, and the evidence of the harm done by habitual TV is piling up elsewhere.

One hypothesis is that the flash-and-dash of the fast-moving screen is throwing the species off its age-old perceptual track by making us passengers in vicarious learning rather than participants in direct experience. The natures of early intellectual and sensory learning and of television communication may be largely incompatible.

LEARNING BY DOING

There are factors in the perceptual development of children that make them quite unready to take on TV viewing as a major experience while they are very young: They need time for reflection in order to absorb and process experience, and they need lots of human interaction in order to learn optimally. The infant cannot learn about things and people through his eyes alone; he must touch them with his hands as well, feel their impact in his palm, and move his fingers over their edges. The outer world remains formless until he can give it shape with experience gained through both his eyes and hands.

One major source of children's direct experience has always been play. Because of the tremendous opportunities for sensory involvement and social interaction involved in play, it is an important building block of perception. Children do not play as much as they used to because they are watching TV, and studies show that children do not tend to watch TV and play at the same time. The decline of play is a serious effect of habitual TV viewing. As a result of the decline of play in early childhood, children have more and more vicarious experience brought to them by TV and less and less real-life experience. They are not as well armed as they should be as they begin to process TV images.

Only after years of direct experiences will the child be able to employ abstract thinking and symbols. While electronic images seem to provide shortcuts to "learning by doing," they cannot replace the sensory play and experimentation that are so critical to the child's development. Even in an age of fast food and instant pudding, things take time.

Consider the following as perceptual exercises:

- Tommy, age three, is standing on an orange crate at the washtub—up to his elbows in water. He sinks his boats, soaks his shirt, and joyously pours water from one plastic food container to another.
- Maria, who is eleven months, is playing peek-a-boo with her father. He holds up a blanket in front of her face, blocking her view of him, and says, "Where's Maria?" She squeals with delight and pulls down the blanket to reveal her whereabouts to her "surprised" father. The game is repeated over and over and this makes it even more fun.
- Carrie and Paul are constructing a neighborhood out of blocks. They build their houses next door to each other; they build a park across the street and, after some discussion, decide to locate the school "over there" near the couch. "I need three more blocks," says one. "The longer one goes on the bottom."
"Two of these are the same as one of those."

While it is easy to see that these children are having fun in their play, they are also developing themselves as learners, increasing the capacity of their imaginations, and developing sociable personalities. These children could not tell us that they are learning important basic concepts: [Through water play, Tommy learns that water can take the shape of its container, that he can mix hot and cold water and make warm, that water has weight and will sink a boat as well as support it.] [Maria, playing peek-a-boo, learns that people exist even when they are out of sight. [Carrie and Paul, the block builders, are practicing eye–hand coordination, solving problems, sensing one object in relation to another.]Beyond this, when they use a block as a stand-in for a fire engine they are learning that one thing can be used to represent another that is not present]This is an essential perceptual step if children are later to understand that letters grouped in words represent real objects and TV images are not "real" but represent real people and things.

Children of all generations have been able to process amazing material in the first three years of life. This is worth noting because many younger parents seem to believe that their children need to watch *Sesame Street* in order to learn numbers and letters and to be prepared for kindergarten. This is simply not the case. More than 20 years before *Sesame Street*, Arnold Gesell and Frances L. Ilg described some normal activities of the typical three-year-old:

> He can repeat three digits; he is beginning to count to three; he enumerates three objects in a picture; he is familiar with three basic forms: circle, square and triangle; he can combine three blocks to build a bridge. Many of his sentences and questions consist of three units. He likes to compare two objects, and this requires a three-step logic.

Gesell and Ilg continue:

> He listens to words with increased assurance and insight. He even likes to make acquaintance with new words, apparently intrigued by their phonetic novelty. He has learned to listen to adults, and he listens to learn from them. He uses words with more confidence and with intelligent inflection, although he may not overcome infantile articulations until the age of four or five. For

practice, he soliloquizes and dramatizes, combining actions and words. He creates dramatic situations to test out
and to apply his words. In this way he extends the range
and depth of his command of language. . . . These action–thought patterns, like his postural patterns, will
come into evidence in his nursery behavior.[2]

All indications point to the young child's sensory style of
learning. Because children experience the world directly, and
do not work with symbols or abstractions as adults do, what
can be easily understood by an adult may not be understood by
a child.

The Swiss psychologist Jean Piaget demonstrated this in a
famous series of experiments. In one demonstration he put on
the table a tall, narrow glass partially filled with water; beside
it he placed a short, wide glass containing the same quantity of
water. Invariably, children under the age of six could not ·
believe that the glasses carried the same amount of water. Even
if they poured the water back and forth, they could not be
comfortable with the idea that certain attributes of an object
(such as mass or weight) can change while others remain the
same.

Lack of experience also affects the way children perceive
words. A kindergarten teacher relates:

> There always comes a time in the kindergarten year when
> we read aloud the book Leo the Late Bloomer, a story
> which says that everybody learns different things at
> different times. I remind them, "Some of us are late to
> learn swimming or late to learn how to walk—and some of
> us are late readers."
> One day a girl spoke up, "Yes, I know my daddy was a
> late reader."
> "Oh, how do you know?"
> "Because he reads till midnight with his light on."

Not all symbols (words) are clarified by their context. The
perception of a phrase such as "late reader" will depend on
the experience of the person who is doing the perceiving.

Experience—or the lack of it—can change the way children look at television in general. In one study a psychologist asked a heterogeneous group of 103 preschoolers the following question: Do you watch TV? What do you watch? Do the people on TV see you? If you wave at them do they wave back? Do the people on TV hear you? If they ask you a question, do the people on TV hear you? If you ask them a question, do they answer you? Virtually all of the three-year-olds thought that the people on TV could see them. About half of the four-year-olds did too.

In addition to their being the result of the child's lack of experience, his perceptions are the product of a natural, physical, "animal" way of relating to the world. The child's method of thinking is "close to the earth." Piaget said that children's thinking is "egocentric," or self-centered. The child sees himself as the cause of happenings and thinks he can control nature, which is alive, as he is. Events that occur together are seen to have a causal relationship. According to Piaget, ('The young child's thought is magical, illogical, animistic, and based on intuition rather than reality. He believes that the moon follows him around, that clouds move in order to bring the night and that mountains grow because stones have been planted." The child's close identification with nature and with animals results from physical factors of size and age, which account also for the way he perceives. "The young child's identification with animals may be stronger than with humans," says Dr. Leopold Bellak. "This is probably why animals are so popular in fables and other children's literature including cartoons." Bellak, creator of the Children's Apperception Test (C.A.T.), says, "In Rorschach Tests, smaller children invariably identify with animals in the ink blots."

Because of these and other elements of youngsters' thinking, children under seven years of age generally don't differentiate fantasy from reality; commercials from programs; heroes from villains; real life from TV; reality from dreams.[3]

To understand what the child perceives via TV, we must examine the kinds of images and ideas that are dispensed by television and learn how these are metabolized by the child. In other words, there are two basic parts to any consideration of learning by television. First we need to examine what the screen brings to the child, then we need to understand *what the child brings to the screen*. The child's perception of TV images will be governed by the accumulation of real-life experience. Because children lack the accumulated experience of adults, what is clear to an adult may not be clear to a child.

Bellak comments:

> Less mature children are likely to tell stories about these pictures [see pp.44 and 45] in which the little mouse is helpless against the lion or the monkey against the tiger. Children with more resources may make up stories that suggest some coping ability of the smaller animal they identify with. The lion, for instance, may bump his head when the mouse disappears into the hole and the tiger may miss as the monkey moves away with agility. In that sense they perceive the pictures differently, in keeping with their higher or lower cognitive development.

LEARNING BY TELEVISION

The nature of the television medium is problematic for the child's perceptual process because it is one-way, instant, and highly visual.

By nature, TV is one-way communication; it talks at you but doesn't hear you. It beams pictures to you but can't see or hear your responses. It requires no interaction. For children— whose natural development depends on learning by doing and on getting a response—this is an unnatural way to learn. On one level it teaches children *not to respond*. Interaction and even isolated "participation" are sharply limited in TV viewing. For example, if Captain Kangaroo should say, "Go find a piece of paper and a crayon," there is no guarantee that the child will follow the direction or be encouraged to do so.

Teachers relate TV viewing to the trouble children now have in responding to verbal directions. One teacher of four-year-olds says:

They don't listen, they tune you out. When you give a simple direction such as, "Please take this down to the art room," many children wouldn't remember what you had just said. The children who have the most trouble following directions often can't repeat short rhymes and have difficulty following clapping patterns.

They don't *expect you* to *expect them* to follow directions. After all, when they're watching TV for all those hundreds of hours they're not asked for a response. It doesn't matter if they give a response because no one will know whether they do or not. That's the key problem with preschool viewing: they don't have to interpret what is said into an action.

The instant, "magical" nature of TV imagery has produced an environment in which images, ideas, and expectations must be satisfied quickly, without explanation. Television's most successful techniques—quick cuts, short segments, fast action, changing camera angles—assault the senses and condition the brain to change. But they inhibit continuity and concentration of thought.

Through camera shifts, called cuts or fades, which occur every few seconds, time is broken into perceptual bits. Each camera shift requires the brain to readjust its perspective and process the image, even though the eyes remain stationery. Dr. Christine Nystrom, psychologist at New York University, explains that these techniques create a variety of "time treatments" that affect us differently. Basically, TV compresses time—squeezes it down into smaller portions than we could ever experience in real life.

> In a TV studio, for example, we have three cameras. When a viewer sees a program that is produced with three cameras—as most programs are—it means that the viewer watching at home doesn't have just one pair of eyes through which to see the situation, but three! He is, in effect, three people, each one viewing the situation from a different angle. The viewer is presented with a greater variety of events . . . or images . . . than would be possible for him or her to see in real life.

Intense visual excitement and stress are thus promoted by television's treatment of time.

Further, the picture on TV changes every five or six seconds, either by changing the camera angle or cutting to an entirely new scene. One researcher refers to these events as "jolts per minute," noting that as time is cut up, the brain is conditioned to change at the expense of continuity of thought.

Adults and children are conditioned to instant gratification and crisis on many levels. David Sontag, vice-president of Prime-Time Television (Twentieth Century Fox), described this condition, which he calls "The Age of Instant."

> Centuries from now when children dial their three dimensional video scanners to the day's history lesson they will learn about the Ages: the Dark Age, the Renaissance Age, the Industrial Age, and the Age of "Instant." . . . The AGE OF INSTANT, which lasted well into the 1980's, was marked by an all-out attempt to make everything instantaneous. There was Instant Coffee, Instant Potatoes, Instant Beef Stew, Instant Pictures (archeologists have uncovered a camera called Instamatic). Everything was standardized then, including job tasks, so that products could be produced quickly, i.e., instantly. This drive to instantize society permeated every level of life. People wore clothing designed to give them instant identification (Brooks Brothers' suits, jeans, the Gucci symbol). They wore their hair for instant identification (short hair . . . long hair). Advertisements urged you to smoke this, drink that, drive this, live here . . . and people will know instantly who you are. Nothing was safe from the onslaught. There were ads proclaiming "Instant Marriages—No Waiting—Open 24 hours a Day." . . . It was right next to one announcing "Instant Divorce; Horseback riding and tennis also available."[4]

"Kids can't wait for anything," says a typical first-grade teacher. "They can't seem to be taught to stand in line, to sit still for a story or to pay attention. This is a pervasive condition."

"As children grow," explained the late Dorothy H. Cohen,

professor of early childhood development at Bank Street College of Education in New York City, "their capacity for attention is heightened by the stability and order they experience in the environment, especially in their relations with significant adults and in orderly contact with the objective world of materials and things. Children whose lives are a kaleidoscope of changing figures and inconsistent responses, for whom things (and people) disappear and fail to reappear with frequency; or children whose environment is heavily dominated by the frantic pace and speed of television, are children likely to be easily distracted. For them, focusing and paying attention are a strain."

Does it matter to children's thinking whether they learn by the language of pictures (TV) rather than by the language of words (books)? Studies suggest that it does. Laurene Meringoff, a researcher at Harvard University's Project Zero, carried out a study in which two groups of preschoolers were presented with two versions of the same story. One group was read the story from a picture book; the other group watched a televised animated version of the book with the text narrated for the soundtrack.

Those who were exposed to the picture book version showed greater recollection of the verbal information in the story and greater understanding of what the story was about. Meringoff and her colleagues say that this is due to the inability of the children in the television group to pay attention to the verbal soundtrack at the same time they are following the visual information. For young children, the continual visual stimulation of television apparently decreases their attention to the verbal story information.

The researchers also found that the discrepancy between understanding of the story was greatest when the child's own knowledge was insufficient to make sense of the events being portrayed visually—that is, when understanding the pictures depended on understanding the verbal information for correct interpretation, or when the verbal information had no visual representation at all.[5]

These studies suggest that how we learn is as important as

what we learn and that TV can seem like a shortcut to perceptual learning but may in fact seriously inhibit it.

REALITY

In a world of vicarious experience, we are not at the mercy of reality—but of what we are told about it, suggested Dr. Bellak in *Overload*. Yet the "world according to TV" and the real world are two quite different places. What TV tells us about violence, sexuality, material goods, and human beings influences our feelings, behaviors, and judgments before we are taught by life experience.

Marie Winn, author of *The Plug-In Drug—Television and the Family*, cautions us to consider "the very nature of the television experience. . . . Perhaps the ever-changing array of sights and sounds coming out of the machine—the wild variety of images meeting the human eye and the barrage of human and inhuman sounds reaching the ear—fosters the illusion of a varied experience for the viewer. It is easy to overlook a deceptively simple fact: one is always *watching television* when one is watching television rather than having any other experience."

Many of the messages coming at children in this vicarious activity come through truncated, instant definitions in the form of stereotypes. Years before television, Walter Lippmann noted that stereotypes provide us with a shortcut for the perceptual process. "The subtlest and most pervasive of all influences are those which create and maintain a repertory of stereotypes. We are told about the world before we see it. We imagine most things before we experience them. And those preconceptions, unless education has made us acutely aware, govern deeply the whole process of perception."[6]

TV provides us with information about "reality" by employing stereotypes. What kinds of messages are coming through? Certainly there is a plethora of stereotypical information about violence, the world of material goods, and about people.

Drs. George Gerbner and Larry Gross head a research team at the Annenberg School of Communication at the University of

Pennsylvania that attempts to identify the differences between the television world and the real world. Their studies show that the world as it is portrayed on TV is far more violent than the real world. In one of their studies they compared the effects of the TV world on the attitudes of heavy viewers (who watched more than four hours a day) and light viewers (who watched two or less hours a day). They found that heavy viewers tended to overestimate their chances of encountering violence. The heavy viewers also reflected more mistrust of others, were more likely to have obtained dogs, locks, guns for protection, and were afraid to walk alone in the city at night.[7]

In another study of seven- to eleven-year-olds, it was shown that two-thirds of the children interviewed were afraid "somebody bad" might get into their houses. Nearly a quarter said they felt afraid of "TV programs where people fight and shoot guns," and heavy watchers were twice as likely to feel "scared often."[8]

In addition, TV gives children an unreal perception of the world of material goods. Like the lesson of violence, the life-style of consumption isn't "taught" by television. It is simply picked up and absorbed by the viewer. Both programs and commercials present an unrealistic view of the material world, one which represents a standard of living that most Americans will never attain. Unfortunately, many children will assume these unreasonable standards to establish their expectations of themselves and to judge their own achievements. Contemporary television families wrestle with unbelievable problems, but their material surroundings can be just as fantastic. Most homes on soap operas have felt the decorator's touch. The house on *Family* is spacious, gracious and well decorated. And one can only marvel at the way the head of the *Eight Is Enough* household keeps his extra-large family in such style in a time of soaring inflation. One series of automobile ads featured people giving new cars to family members as gifts for such special occasions as an anniversary, a graduation, and a sixteenth birthday.

 If the television version of reality is used by our children as a basis for their judgments of the material world, we have cause for concern; if they use television images to judge other people, we are in deep trouble, given the power and importance the television world confers on certain categories of people and the way in which it denies them to others.

What is unsettling is the ease with which most people believe the stereotypes of people on TV. A group's representation on TV—or lack of it—conveys a message about that group's importance in society. Women, for example, make up over 50 percent of the population, yet they comprise about 25 percent of the characters on prime-time television. White males fill over 60 percent of the roles, although they actually represent about 40 percent of the population. The percentage of women of color on TV is less than half that in real life.[9] Children's programming reflects the same biases, as has been shown in the content analyses done by Dr. F. Earle Barcus at Boston University (see Chapter 7, "The Effects on Social Relationships").

TV AND IMAGINATION

Habitual TV viewing denies the imagination the opportunity to flourish by its usual means. At home few children know the privilege of boredom—which could yield fanciful ideas—because television is encouraged to fill in any available space. In our fact-oriented, TV-saturated society, too often make-believe, pretending, and imaginative play are considered frivolous or diversionary activity—therefore unimportant. Even the books that are chosen for children by adults reveal our tendency toward facts versus fantasy. Fanciful times in the land of Oz or trips in rhyme or poetry are passed up for a story about *Jane's Day at the Dentist* or *Let's Visit the Airport*.

Daydreaming and imaginative play promote the child's perceptual maturity, emotional growth, and creative development in ways that television does not. Imagination is the capacity of the mind to project itself beyond its own perceptions and sensations; it is a capacity we are all born with, but it must be given encouragement and opportunity if it is to develop fully. Fantasy—a flower of the imagination—serves a vital purpose for a child and requires time away from the TV in order to grow. Fantasy should be part of the child's real world. The young child is actively engaged in a struggle to become a rational, mature human being; he has relatively little knowledge of how the world works and may use fantasy to fill in the gaps in his knowledge. He peoples his world with creatures, monsters, and "wild things" to explain the phenomena that he can't understand, such as shadows in the darkness or thunder on a stormy night. At the same time he gains a better understanding of his inner self. Unconscious fears and anxieties are externalized through fantasy and make-believe play. Having detached himself, the child can examine, understand, and put them in perspective.[10]

Make-believe enters the child's world as early as 18 months, when he may pretend to drink from an empty cup. Before long, as his powers of imagery grow, the child will be able to drink with no props at all. The image of the cup he holds in his mind will be sufficient. Make-believe reaches its peak in the preschool years between two and four years of age and remains a major part of the child's intellectual life until age seven or eight when it gives way to structured games and daydreaming. The overall benefits of this period, however, remain throughout adulthood. Ironically, the prime time for the development of imagination—between ages four and seven—is precisely the time when children's minds are most captured by TV viewing.

Drs. Dorothy and Jerome Singer, psychologists at the Family and Television Research Center at Yale University, conclude:

> Fantasy and make-believe play increase ability to explore new contexts and to try out new situations in odd combinations. This exploration of novelty makes children sensitive to the creativity of others as expressed in stories, or movies or art. It also lays the groundwork for their own creative development. It has been shown that men and women who demonstrated creative achievements early in their lives had engaged in a good deal of fantasy as children, and often developed imaginary companions.

They had also been exposed to considerable storytelling by their parents, or played pantomime games with them.[11]

While television hasn't killed the imagination, it has hurt it. It occupies the child's mind and time, limiting the opportunities for the child to exercise his imagination. Flights of fantasy take off from real life experiences, fueled by the capacity to create pictures in the mind. Before Kung Fu, Batman, and bionics hit the scene, kindergarten children relied more on their own experiences as material for make-believe play. When they weren't handed prepackaged fantasies, they spun their own.

Imaginative play still occurs, and the universal plots of play still appear, including themes of healing ("doctor"), protecting ("house"), taking a trip, and more. It is of great concern to teachers, however, that today's kids don't play nearly as much—and they don't seem to know how to play. When children do play, it is a very different kind of behavior—copied straight from the TV screen. "Children are presenting very poor fantasy material . . . very little comes from inside." One teacher describes it:

> We all remember the first big influence of TV in the nursery schools, when Batman play swept the classrooms and diverted large numbers of children from materials and other forms of imaginative play. The Batman play had a compulsive character to it, as though the children could not stop. When teachers finally stopped reeling from the impact, many put limits on Batman play and insisted that the children turn to other themes and to enjoyment of variety in materials.

To the child who watches them on TV, Bionic Woman and Batman appear to have spectacular powers, but as models for play their range is limited. The child has a need to release his native imagery, but, alas, it may not fit the Batman mold.

TV also delivers incessant commercial messages about *toys*, which highly influence choices for the object of play. Toys are the tools of play that shape and structure children's imaginings. A tricycle suggests one type of play, "Baby Tender Love" another, a Shogun Warrior still another, a tub of water yet another.

In one study, children were given an opportunity to play with both highly structured toys (those with a definite identity suggesting a specific function, such as a Batman cape) and minimally structured toys (those with vague identities that could be used in various ways, such as a rope or blocks). All the children produced a greater variety of play themes in response to the unstructured toys.[12]

Toys can range from a cardboard box, a clothespin, or a rubber ball to a mouse that marches, a cow that gives milk, or a battery-operated doll.

The toys advertised on TV are clearly of the second variety and frequently battery-operated. They are designed to meet the economic needs of adult advertisers rather than the developmental needs of children; that is, they are designed to sell. TV toys are those that look the best on television. They tend to be colorful, highly structured action toys.

Dolls modeled after TV characters suggest play that is limited by the behavior of those characters on television. The Fonzie doll is not likely to be used as a knight or cowboy. The owner of a Barbie Doll with an extensive wardrobe will probably spend a great deal of time dressing and undressing the doll. A battery-operated train zooming around a small plastic track leaves the child with little to do besides operating the on/off switch and watching. Such toys leave far less room for the child's imagination to wander than a cardboard box that might become a boat or a doll's bed, a hut or a hotel, a spaceship or a shopping cart. But have you ever seen a cardboard box advertised on TV?

The effects of TV on perception are further scrambled by children's inability to distinguish what is real and unreal (or imaginary) on the screen. It usually does not occur to the younger child to ask, "What is real?" and "What isn't?" The older child may ask the question and arrive at a point of regarding a program as a "show" involving "stars"—while still feeling unconsciously that it is essentially "true," telling it "like it is."

Even adults sometimes have trouble understanding what is real or unreal on TV, as illustrated by their subsequent behaviors. Each year Dr. Marcus Welby, a TV doctor played by Robert Young, gets thousands of letters from viewers asking him for medical advice. Erik Barnouw explains this "absorption in the symbolic process":

> In drama there appear to be people in almost every audience who never quite fully realize that a play (or program) is a set of fictional, symbolic representations. An actor is one who symbolizes other people. In a movie, some years ago, Frederic March enacted with great skill the role of a drunkard. Florence Eldridge (Mrs. March) reports that for a long time thereafter she got letters of advice and sympathy from women who said they too were married to alcoholics. Also, some years ago it was reported that when Edward G. Robinson, who played gangster roles with extraordinary vividness, visited Chicago, local hoodlums would telephone him at his hotel to pay their professional respects.[13]

This kind of absorption in the symbolic process, plus their shortage of knowledge about the real world, leave children generally vulnerable to fearful situations that an older viewer might pass off as foolish, fantastic, and wholly vicarious. (See Chapter 6, "The Promotion of Aggressive Behavior.") Children do not necessarily know that Godzilla is a miniature model invented for the screen and embellished by camera techniques. If their own monsters seem real to them, why not this one too, who looks and acts so lifelike? We are talking now about young children (who watch Godzilla, etc.) and who will answer the TV set or wave back at a character who waves at them. These are the children who don't differentiate very well between animation and live action or between programs and commercials.

It is not necessary for all the material used for fantasy to come from within the child. Children can benefit from the influence of real-life adults or the stimulation of literature. Dr. Bruno Bettelheim, internationally recognized psychologist and author of *The Uses of Enchantment,* advocates that fairy tales be read aloud, enabling the child to obtain from them clues to fantasies that relate directly to his inner conflicts. Bettelheim believes that they offer the child positive ways of resolving those conflicts in fantasies that children recycle with their own.

Bettelheim would probably be very upset to see all of the fairy tales translated to television forms. The reason that fairy tales "work" in the mind is that the child receives the image *in words* and then must conjure up and fill out that image according to his needs and experience. Both print and radio leave part of the image unfinished; the visual information has to be supplied by the receiver's imagination. Children who listened to the Lone Ranger on radio would each have a slightly different view of his appearance and the settings for his adventures. In their mental processes they would embellish his costume and create his facial features. Similarly, when a story is read by a child or read aloud to the child by an adult, visualization of the characters and events is left mostly to the child's imagination. Even if the book is illustrated, it does not show every scene nor provide the action. Central to this need to use the imagination is the fact that the violence in books or on radio can only be as fierce as the child's experience will allow; in some measure the child is protected by his inexperience.

By contrast, few inferences are made while watching television. TV delivers all of the images to us and therefore we do not participate in the inner picture-making activity. TV "fantasy" comes ready-made by adults; the pictures all come from outside rather than from inside the child.

Another drawback to television is that it does not allow for "stopping in the middle," repeating, or taking time to digest or understand the pictures and words. A good story in print will take on new shades of meaning with each rereading, and the person can pause or go back if more time is required to assimilate the material.

Children today are losing their ability to make their own

mental pictures. "I can't hear it without pictures," says the child.

THE BRIGHTER SIDE

Well aware of the dampening effects of TV on the imagination, Drs. Dorothy and Jerome Singer, at the Yale Family Television Research and Consultation Center, are trying to teach parents and teachers how to use their children's viewing experiences to improve the imagination. They have said that sometimes television can stimulate the child by suggesting plots, themes, and characters for make-believe play: "If anything, television has probably increased the likelihood of imaginative play for many children who otherwise might not have been provided with the variety of material that becomes the basis of assimilation." They say that this is especially true for the poor, for whom TV has "widened the horizons" of raw material for make-believe.

However, the Singers qualify their endorsement somewhat, saying that to be of benefit, television programs should be at the child's level of understanding and that parents should participate in what their children watch. Moreover, the Singers notably preface their endorsement of TV as a learning tool by saying that they recommend no TV viewing in the preschool years and limited amounts until the child has developed good reading habits. They caution that the child should not become habituated to the easy-come "learning" of TV; reading requires more effort on the part of the learner.

Mindful of the need for moderation, the Singers set out to determine if watching Mr. Rogers' would affect children's play. They systematically observed four groups of children at play, each group having had a different kind of experience with Mr. Rogers'.

The first group watched the program every day for two weeks, unaccompanied by adults or others.

The second group also watched for two weeks, with an adult mediating the program's imaginative content. This meant reinforcing imaginative ideas and encouraging play that would help the child "rehearse" the make-believe behaviors.

A third group watched no TV at all but spent the same time with a teacher who engaged them in activities involving make-believe and imagination.

A fourth group watched no television and received no special attention.

The children exposed to the live adult and no TV at all showed the greatest increase in pretend play and imagination. Those who watched the program with the adult facilitator showed the next greatest gains. The two groups receiving no adult attention showed little or no gains in their imaginative play.[14]

The study points up a key role that parents can play, that of a "model" for imaginative activity. Parents can initiate and encourage make-believe play even in babies. Games as simple as "This Little Piggy" introduce the first elements of make-believe. Later a parent—or any adult—can suggest themes and provide props for make-believe. Sometimes an adult can provide a model while pursuing his or her own imaginative activity even though the child is not directly involved.

It is natural that adults celebrate and share in the early learning of the young. If we want the next generation to be alert, caring, hopeful, and wise, we should be asking how we can best use television to meet some of children's basic learning needs: to be able to trust, to learn by doing, to have reasonable information about reality, to develop and exercise their imaginations, to be well nourished in both mind and body.

■ 4 ■
THE
EFFECTS
ON
READING

Nothing yet invented
meets the intellectual needs
of the human brain so fully as print.
The ability of the mind
to convert little markings on paper
into meaning is one of the ways
civilization receives its basic energy.

Norman Cousins

"I don't want to read it, I want to *see it in real pictures,*" says young John. Raised on the language of pictures, today's children see little in print, the written language of words. Yet even in this age of instant replay and satellite hookups, children still have a basic need to read.

By age seven or eight a youngster needs to read in order to participate in the daily life of the community, to succeed in school, and to meet the expectations of family, teachers, neighbors, and peers. During the later school years almost 90 percent of a student's work depends directly on reading ability. The student who fails to develop a highly skilled reading ability will face a serious handicap. The more obvious disadvantages of being a poor reader include failure in school, the prospect of a less rewarding job, lower lifetime earnings, reduced social status, and less joy and spontaneity in lifelong learning. The semiliterate person does not have access to the richness that is to be gained through reading literature, poetry, history, and philosophy. As Professor Neil Postman of New York University put it in his book, *Teaching as a Conserving Activity:*

> . . . to become educated means to become aware of the origins and growth of knowledge and knowledge systems; to be familiar with the intellectual and creative processes by which the best that has been thought and said has been produced. . . . For to know about your roots is not merely to know where your grandfather came from, and what he had to endure. It is also to know where your ideas come from, and why you happen to believe them; and to know where your moral and aesthetic sensibility comes from. It is to know where your world, not just your family, comes from.

None of this is possible without reading. It is not surprising then that, in a society of print-based institutions, lack of reading ability has been closely associated with low self-esteem and sometimes antisocial behavior. In the United States the child who does not read by about age eight feels inadequate. As a result, problems develop, and even when the problems are not severe the sensitivities are real. Eight-year-old John began to sob one evening at bedtime and told his mother, "I'm the worst reader in the class and everybody knows it!" This was not really the case, but John felt that it was. His mother pointed out that his friends say he's the best soccer player on the team. "I don't care," he blurted, "I don't want to be good at sports, I want to be good at school!"

Being good at school means being good at reading. And, fairly or unfairly, the school's success is evaluated by local reading levels. To meet the generally perceived need to read, we produce more reading material in the form of books, kits, and toys and more reading teachers than any other country.

Even so—and to our increasing dismay—we are spawning a

generation of semiliterates: 14 percent of entering kindergar-
teners have diagnosed reading/learning disabilities; 60 percent
of New York City's public school students read below the
national norm, and an increasing portion of college freshmen
must take remedial writing courses in order to do normal
college work. In spite of growing awareness, downward trends
in the reading/writing spiral continue along with increasing
concern for the future of democratic institutions as we know
them. People ask: "If print survives, who will use it? Everybody? Or a shrinking elite?" As one linguist, Wendell Johnson,
has written:

> If the effective use of language cannot be taught . . . we
> may well have occasion to despair of the grand experi-
> ment dreamed by Voltaire, championed by Washington
> and Franklin, and cherished by the American people
> through many generations. And if we despair of that, then
> truly, even if you do learn to speak correct English, it may
> well not seem to matter very much "who you talk it to."
> For when people cannot adequately speak or write their
> language, there arise strong men to speak it for them—and
> "at" them.

Eventually children need to read much more than stop signs
and cereal labels and to write more than spelling lists. But a
survey of what's happening suggests that there is no longer the
traditional reverence for reading that existed prior to the
development of television as an integral part of our daily lives.

PRESCHOOL EXPERIENCE DECLINING

Each year children read less and less and watch television
more and more. In fact, Americans of all ages watch more
television each year. The typical child sits in front of the
television about four hours a day—and for children in lower
socioeconomic families the amount of time thus spent is even
greater. In either case, the child spends more time with TV
than he or she spends talking to parents, playing with peers,
attending school, or reading books. TV time usurps family

time, play time, and the reading time that could promote language development.⌋

⌊Babies and very young children are not read to or talked to as much as in former times. Verbal activities—from peek-a-boo and patty-cake to nursery rhymes, songs, bedtime stories, and dinner table talk—tend to be sacrificed for the convenience of easy entertainment via television.⌡Yet major studies have shown that children who have been read to during their preschool years are more likely than others to be successful in meeting the verbal requirements of the classroom and in learning to read.⌡ In one experiment in which lower-class mothers were paid to read aloud to their infants for at least ten minutes a day, the children forged ahead of the control group and showed significant differences in all phases of speech by twenty months of age.[2] In another experiment carried out in seven schools in New York City with socially disadvantaged second-graders, the students whose teachers read aloud to them daily showed impressive gains in reading interest and ability.[3]

POOR ATTENTION SPAN

❧ As mentioned in previous chapters, children entering kindergarten today exhibit markedly diminished listening skills and attention spans. Both are closely associated with the development of reading skills. The ability to pay attention is a primary element in all thinking. But hundreds of long-time teachers say that today's five-year-olds cannot pay attention as well as five-year-olds did only ten years ago. The child who cannot pay attention and who is forever fidgeting, dreaming, shifting, and squirming is not manifesting reading readiness.

Generally, the capacity to pay attention is enhanced by maturity and heightened by stability and order in the environment. Because this was also true in the past (when children paid attention better), we should look for new elements in modern childhood and examine their effects. Television viewing is the most obvious new and major factor because it is children's primary waking activity. Television's most success-ful techniques—short segments, fast action, quick cuts, fades, dissolves—break time into perceptual bits. Reading requires perceptual continuity to track line after line. Television habituates the mind to short takes, not to the continuity of thought required by reading. The pace and speed of television cause children to be easily distracted; they are inundated with too many messages and cannot stop to make sense of this confusion. Focusing and paying attention to print become an unnatural strain for the conditioned TV viewer.

The very entertainment techniques that produce the pace and polish of successful television programming often create a negative influence on the child's motivation to read. Increasingly, the TV child wants to be entertained in school. He demands entertainment in the razzle-dazzle ways of the TV screen or he turns off. The teacher would have to be as quick, fast-paced, and full of flashiness as the child's TV—with a constantly changing bag of materials, jokes, and costumes. Obviously, this is not the way reading can be taught. A teacher says, "I can't compete with television. I can't change my body into different letters, nor can I change color. The lessons I consider exciting fall flat because I don't do these phenomenal things."

READING PROBLEMS INCREASING

As print takes a backseat to television, reading difficulties in the grade schools are increasing. Elementary school teachers who have taught for 15 years or more report that while more children come to school knowing letter names and number names, the same children have increasing difficulty processing language. They don't talk, read, comprehend, listen, or write as well as they would have been expected to 15 years ago. Even if *Sesame Street* gets children started on learning letters by rote, many fail to make the leap from *recognition* of letters and sounds into *reading* during the second or third grade. "Premature learning" may be the reason, according to the late Dr. Dorothy H. Cohen. "A more

careful assessment of individual readiness, not in terms of age,
grade or adult anxiety, but in terms of the specific kinds of
maturity required, could avoid a good deal of reading failure with
all the concomitant emotional and societal upheaval that goes
with such failure."

\The teachers' reports concur with news that diagnosed
reading disabilities are on the increase, SAT scores are falling,
increasing numbers of college entrants need remedial reading
and writing courses, and an alarming number of young
mothers cannot read well enough to read traditional children's
books aloud to their young.

TV viewing has been correlated with poor reading ability
and low IQ in two separate studies by Michael Morgan and
Larry Gross at the Annenberg School of Communication at the
University of Pennsylvania, and by Drs. Dorothy and Jerome
Singer at Yale University. When Morgan and Gross studied
625 public school students in the sixth through ninth grades in
suburban/rural New Jersey, they found that those who watched
a great deal of television had the poorer reading ability. They
do not, however, suggest that they are presenting a simple
cause-and-effect model.

[Children who either have "reading problems," or who
find reading to be frustrating, intimidating, or simply
boring may more often seek fantasy stimulation and
entertainment from television.]Although we find that the
amount of television viewing will predict a student's
reading comprehension score better than many other
variables, the notion that television has singlehandedly
caused poor performance cannot be substantiated, at least
on the basis of the present data. Television may serve to
reinforce a reading problem, to be sure, in the sense that
while a student is watching TV, he or she is not fully
concentrating on reading; or heavy viewing may merely be
symptomatic of that problem.

Psychologists Dorothy and Jerome Singer reported similar
findings in their studies at Yale University.

DECLINE IN LIBRARY USE

At the same time that teachers are reporting a decline in reading skills among school children, librarians lament the drop in circulation of children's books. The national association of librarians reports about a 15 percent decrease in circulation in children's libraries during the last decade. The study is based on a random sample of public libraries in the United States serving communities of at least 25,000 people. Despite heroic efforts to provide story hours and to adapt book collections to the interests of children, these lures have not altered the trend away from the library.

Even children who can read do not choose to read for pleasure. Adults despair that although children know how to read, they just don't do so unless it is required. For example, Adam is a precocious nine-year-old who is part of the school's program for the gifted. His mother notes that he never reads anything that is not an assignment. When the school librarian is there to encourage him, Adam will phlegmatically "choose" a "nonbook," perhaps a catalog, book of lists, or anthology of jokes. He'll usually change reading material many times in the course of a library period at school, reading a page here and a paragraph there—similar to the way he flips the TV dial.

Television—not print—is the children's literature of our times. Most of today's school children have not read the books that their teachers studied in "children's literature" courses in college, nor do they know fairy tales and nursery rhymes as did former generations. They know TV programs better than books, and when they do read books they are mostly poorly written items about TV monsters, robots, etc. Their literature is electronic, and is written primarily in the language of pictures, not words.

In addition, the words and sentences that children absorb from TV programs are much simpler than the language of books. Books present a broader vocabulary and greater frequency of complex sentences. Professor Adele Fasick at the University of Toronto has shown that the language of children's books consistently offers wider vocabulary as well as more varied and complicated sentence patterns than does television. In fact, the most predominant form on TV is the *incomplete* sentence.[4] The author notes:

> The apparently differing effects of television and reading on children's language learning may be related to the following linguistic factors. First, the great differences in the complexity of language in the various picture books makes possible a closer match between a child and a book than could be made between a child and a television program. The cartoons presented on television are geared to appeal to the widest possible age range. Preschool children have to listen to the same kind of language as their older brothers and sisters. But books are widely varied, presenting language experiences appropriate for children from the time they first start talking to the time when their language is syntactically similar to adult speech. Many of the sentences in the books are more complicated than the sentences heard on television programs. . . . Hearing the complicated language of storybooks, which utilizes most of the syntactic possibilities of English, may help children to understand and to use the more complicated language they will have to employ in school.

CAN TV TEACH READING?

Teachers, parents, and TV producers have tried to find out if we can employ TV to teach reading—or any of the component skills that lead to reading. Can we use the language of pictures to teach the language of words?

Some years ago Marshall McLuhan predicted that the days of print literacy are numbered as we move to electronic media. This may not necessarily be true, as we have seen other media adapt to new conditions. For example, people feared that the "big bands" would die when phonograph records were invented, but instead the bands became the major programming for the recording industry. Then the recording industry was threatened by radio, so records became the major programming for radio. Then TV threatened to kill radio and radio responded with new formats—the "single sound" of "all news," "all rock," "all country." Now TV threatens print. TV will, no doubt, alter both books and readers. But, as Norman Cousins has said, "We are confident that print will not only endure but will continue to be a primary force in the life of the mind."

For the child, the natural style of television presents serious competition to print and reading, and obviously there are inherent conflicts between learning by print and learning by television. First, compared with the passive intake of television, reading is hard, analytical work for the child. Much effort and practice go into learning letter sounds and then letter names, then linking letters in blends or other combinations, and finally putting them together until they make syllables, words, sentences, paragraphs, and meaning. Reading requires effort and practice, while sitting immobile before the TV set does not. Watching television, however, also does not develop habits of initiative, analysis, or close attention to the printed page.

Second, when human eyes read a line of print they see letters—little black marks—one after the next in long, straight, parallel lines. To gather meaning, eyes move from left to right. The image on the TV screen is produced and perceived in a completely different way. Pictures exist as a constantly moving field of winking dots in a see-through grid. It's quite possible that left–right eye habits employed in reading are unconsciously eroded by several hours a day of watching television. The eye and brain functions employed in TV viewing likely put demands on different parts of the brain than those used in reading, causing incalculably different kinds of cognitive development at the expense of reading and writing aptitudes. What we do know from experience is that children read less easily and with less pleasure than they used to only a few short years ago.

Our sense of the probable incompatibility of television and reading perception is based on the known facts about how the left and right hemispheres of the brain function. The left hemisphere is the source of most of our language power (i.e., the language of words). The left side is associated with the capacity to speak, write, read, count, compute, and reason. It is the hemisphere that "puts things in order," then adds them up. This capacity is necessary when the brain perceives printed letters, scans them, and joins them to make meaning. Damage to the left hemisphere of the brain will usually damage these speaking and reading abilities.

The right side of the brain works in a different way: It perceives the world holistically rather than through analytical structures. It works through pattern recognition, which is the antithesis of the coding and decoding process of the left brain. Professor Neil Postman has written:

> In recognizing a human face, or a picture of it, or anything that requires an "all at once" perception, such as watching TV, we are largely using the right hemisphere of the brain, the left possibly being something of a burden in the process. Thus, continuous TV watching over centuries would conceivably have the effect of weakening left-brain activity, and producing a population of "right-brained" people.

This suggests that habitual TV viewing may be counterproductive to analytical thinking and the mental process needed for reading. It appears that it is not efficient to use the language of television pictures to teach the language of words. Television is primarily the language of pictures, apprehended through right-brain pattern recognition. Books are primarily the language of words, comprehended through left-brain analytical functions.

A third conflict, as discussed earlier, involves the fact that in TV viewing all the pictures are delivered "ready-made" to the viewer; he no longer has to create them. The distinguishing element of both story books and radio is that they operate in the "theater of the mind," on pictures that are made up inside the child. This inner-picture making is an extremely important part of the development of the imagination, listening skill, and reading ability. But today's children frequently do not like story hour; they squirm and complain and do not understand, because "you can't see anything."

SESAME STREET

Considering the immense impact of television, many educators have felt it imperative to try to harness the power of the TV medium to help solve the decline of print literacy and, indeed, a variety of other problems. Can TV be adapted to teach reading? Can it promote interest in reading and words that might carry over to other linguistic activities?

Some of the earliest TV shows aimed at cognitive development. In 1951 Dr. Frances Horwich tried to develop a "nursery school of the air" called *Ding Dong School*. Though exceedingly schoolmarmish, it supplanted a parade of pie-throwing programs and remained on the air until 1959. *Captain Kangaroo* (1955–present) and *Mister Rogers' Neighborhood* (1960–present) both introduce new vocabulary and read books aloud on the air.

But the most overtly instructional program of all, *Sesame Street*, premiered on PBS in 1969 after three years of planning and research. Produced by Children's Television Workshop (CTW), under the leadership of its president, Joan Cooney, *Sesame Street* was developed to raise the level of literacy skills (or readiness for them) in children of poor urban families before they enter kindergarten. Understanding children's strong attraction to TV, and their attraction to commercials, *Sesame* provided the preschool audience with lively entertainment, employing a magazine format and the production techniques used in advertising—fast pace, quick cuts, camera angles, and animation. Establishing its continuity from recurrent formats (such as a street scene and games like "One of These Things Is Not Like the Other"), the series intermingled a cast of real adults and children with Muppets, animation, and live-action film segments.

The revolutionary show won an instant audience of 9.5 million children and demonstrated the power of TV to gather together an entire society of children for the purpose of

teaching a specific skill—in this case, letters and numbers.
→ The issue now beginning to be raised is that *Sesame Street's*
negative side effects may outweigh the benefits of being able to
recite the ABC's at age four. Specifically, *Sesame Street* has
been charged with bombarding toddlers with a superfast
environment they cannot really handle. Critics say that
Sesame pushes cognitive skills at the expense of other values
and prizes rote learning at the expense of thinking. They
charge that *Sesame*, because its production style is based on
short segments and quick cuts, never requires that an attention
span develop and therefore precludes the emergence of a
perceptual reading-readiness state. Further, critics object to
the use of slang, the slapstick and irreverent rewriting of
traditional stories and rhymes, and the presentation of symbols to the very young. Finally, they object to *Sesame's*
popularity itself, sensing that it promotes the "TV habit" at a
young age.

In the context of the problem of language development, we
must assess the producers' ambitions and the critics' complaints with common sense. If children suffer from fast-paced
commercial-style TV, it is not because of *Sesame Street* alone
but because of the cumulative effect of excessive viewing in
general. If children who are unready to learn feel pressed
(consciously or unconsciously) to deal with symbols such as
letters and numbers, that feeling is most likely generated from
the emotional charge in the adults in the household rather
than by a one-way stimulus of the TV medium.

Sesame Street does not and cannot teach reading per se, to
its audience. What it can and does teach (to the child who is
perceptually and emotionally ready) is letter recognition
(ABC's), other-pattern recognition (triangle, square, etc.), and
some sense of continuity through recurrent formats.

Amazingly, traditional theories of learning and instruction
have almost nothing to say about the potential role of formats
in the facilitation of learning, yet the use of recurrent formats
may be an important kind of "pattern recognition" offered to
the regular viewer over time. Dr. Edward Palmer, director of
research at CTW, explains that recurrent formats are the

"workhorses" of children's TV programs in that they carry a large portion of the instruction offered through them. For the television producer, the recurrent use of formats relieves the need to create an entirely new setting, cast of characters, and set of graphics for each. Could it be that recurrent TV formats offer a kind of right-brain pattern continuity—a structure inside which other awarenesses occur?

For example, *Sesame Street* frequently employs a particular recurrent format in its presentation of "sorting" skills. The format contains two main elements. One is a graphic display divided into quadrants, in which four items appear. Three of these are always identical, while one differs from the first three in size, shape, number, class, or function. The second main element is a song that begins, "One of these things is not like the others. . . ."

When children are exposed to this sorting format repeatedly they develop an understanding of the "game" of sorting which transcends a mere understanding of the response that is sought in any particular situation in which the sorting format appears. According to Dr. Palmer, "The child gradually *learns how to learn* from this format, and finally may become quite proficient in grasping and coping with its nuances. When this happens, we may say that the child has developed a facility, or wisdom, in the given format." Seemingly, understanding how formats work may be a significant building block toward reading, where each letter sound operates in the "format" or context of a word, and the word within the sentence. Therefore, pattern recognition (a right-brain function that can be taught by television) would seem to *assist* reading (a left-brain skill that must be learned through print).

However television might help lead a child to reading, a caring adult can do even more. Adults can reinforce the potential positive effects of programs such as *Sesame Street, Captain Kangaroo,* and *Mr. Rogers' Neighborhood* by postponing the regular viewing of them until age four or five, by limiting viewing to one hour a day at the most, by reading aloud to the young child several times a day, by helping the child to memorize traditional nursery rhymes or other verses, and by engaging in lots of conversation and direct experience together.

THE ELECTRIC COMPANY

The Electric Company (Sesame's "sequel") was created by CTW to teach reading skills to second-, third-, and fourth-graders who were having reading difficulties. Aired daily for a half hour and employing technically sophisticated techniques in a humorous action format, *The Electric Company* curriculum emphasized "decoding" skills, particularly three strategies for letter–sound analysis:

- *blending,* which is a sounding-out process for constructing words from smaller parts, sometimes making word families as in "mop," "top," and "pop";
- *chunking,* which is sight recognition of groups of letters as single units, such as "ow," "ight," "th," and "ai";
- *scanning,* which involves looking ahead in a word for spelling patterns that affect pronunciation, such as the silent *e* which dictates that the previous vowel be long.

It is hard to explain *The Electric Company* style and verve to someone who has not watched the show, so viewing it should be every adult's homework. The concepts, letters, and words are presented by everything from rock-and-roll singers, dancers, and musicians to a gorilla and an animated alphabet. Typical of *The Electric Company's* gag vignettes is an episode called, "The Six-Dollar and Thirty-Nine Cent Man," starring Steve Awesome, a hero whose "macrobionic" eyesight enables him to look at a message and project it in big print onto the TV screen.

Through research and testing CTW made some discoveries concerning how to present print on the TV screen. Using apparatus that reflects a beam of light off the cornea of the eye into the camera, Palmer and his staff studied children while they watched proposed segments of the show. Palmer explains:

> You can look through a camera and find where a child's
> eye is focused on the screen, within the space of a dime.
> That testing helped us to determine how much print to
> put on the screen, how many different words and letters,
> what size, where to place them on the screen and how
> long to leave them on the screen. All this, in order to
> maximize the chance that the child will read it.

In these studies researchers learned that the most desirable placing for print is the top one-third of the screen. When possible, print should also be made "part of the action," using it as though it were another actor. "We began to have the actors refer to the print on the screen and even point to it," said one researcher. When a face with clearly defined features appears together with print on the screen, the children's eyes will invariably focus on the faces. However, when silhouettes of heads are shown with printed letters or words coming out of the mouths, children will attend to the print. Another device to prompt attention to print on the screen was discovered when the hero Spiderman was introduced as a component on *The Electric Company*. Spiderman did not talk on the program, but what he was thinking appeared in print inside a balloon over his head, as in the graphic style of a comic book. Tests showed that the balloon device was a most successful way to get kids to read print on the screen.

Research by Educational Testing Service (ETS) in 100 classrooms divided a random sample into viewing and nonviewing classes. Children who watched a single season of *The Electric Company* showed gains in reading skills in comparison to nonviewers. This was especially true for the "target" audience of second-graders who were in the lower half of their class in reading achievement. The greatest gain was for those who watched only one year; those who viewed the show for two years did not seem to gain much more than those who viewed it for one.

The question remains, is TV the medium with which to teach print? Are the returns worth the investment? What if each half-hour spent watching *The Electric Company* had been used in some other form of reading instruction? It seems likely that *The Electric Company* can assist the teacher and pupil whose basic reading program is based on print material, especially when the teacher understands that the value in the *Electric* segments is essentially supplemental. The learning of reading depends on the relationship of teacher and student (and dozens of other factors); and, finally, the mastery of print depends on the relationship of reader and books, and repeated *practice.*

SPIN-OFFS FOR PRINT

Television programs sometimes act as a catalyst or springboard to reading by developing new interests in the viewer. Children frequently select reading material because they associate it with a TV program they have seen. For example, when *The Hardy Boys* became a TV hit, sales for *The Hardy Boys* books jumped dramatically. And when Captain Kangaroo reads one of his "regular" books, such as *Stone Soup* or *Mike Mulligan and His Steam Shovel*, on the air, there is a rush on local libraries for copies of that particular book. Similarly, the TV versions of *The Little House on the Prairie, Roots, The Ascent of Man,* and *I, Claudius* all promoted gains in book sales and suggest the usefulness of TV as a springboard to reading at various levels.

Networks and other private businesses are creating teacher's guides, games, gadgets, and reading curriculums in what amounts to a multimillion-dollar materials boom. All of these materials are coordinated with TV programs and viewing activities and are distributed to teachers and librarians with directions as to how to promote reading and thinking. Study guides have been developed for such programs as *Roll of Thunder, Hear My Cry, Eleanor and Franklin,* and the rebroadcast of *Roots.*

A *Roots II* program for educators was developed by ABC

because of the belief that the script of a TV production would be a valuable and appealing way to teach reading. The Associated Press agreed to an unprecedented distribution of scripts of the first two-hour program to newspapers throughout the country. *Roots II* information kits, which included posters, plot summaries, feature materials, photographs, and a family-tree poster, were sent to more than 2,000 secondary school librarians in the American Library Association and to publishers of educational periodicals. According to research by the National Education Association (NEA), an estimated 20 million students watched *Roots II* as part of a classroom assignment.

This trend has its critics who believe that the TV world is not the milieu for a reading lesson. One educational consultant and TV producer says, "A TV script is one of the most difficult kinds of reading matter to comprehend—even for me with a graduate degree in English literature!" We have seen many bandwagons in the teaching of reading in the last 20 years, from phonics, to "look-say," to ITA. Teaching reading via TV is merely the latest. It will find its cult, polarize educators for a while, paralyze a few students, stimulate others, and modify its practice in the next generation.

Reading remains a process larger than the sum of its parts. When television is used in highly selective ways it can teach some of the subparts: If TV creates a sense of wonder about the unfamiliar, it may promote reading readiness; and if television teaches how to pronounce a consonant blend, it may add something to the total process. But if TV takes away the need to imagine or to analyze, something is subtracted.

[The indispensable element in learning to read is *practice*—and this television can't contribute. If TV viewing time usurps potential reading time, it precludes practice, habit, and skill. And if TV knocks out other building blocks of reading, such as conversation, listening, or play, viewing that takes up reading time should be re-evaluated.]

Critics cannot yet agree on whether television and print can work together. Joan Cooney, president of CTW, has written: "The jury is still out on whether American society (in which an estimated 25 million citizens are functionally illiterate) will marshal sufficient resources to achieve universal literacy. But this much we have learned—the medium of television is one of these resources."

One more skeptical member of that jury is the linguist Wendell Johnson, who pointed out that the trouble with television is that you can't read it. And as essayist E. B. White said about the general deterioration of writing skills, "Short of throwing away all the television sets, I really don't know what you can do about writing."

While that jury is still out, the millions of children who more than ever need to know how to read well are watching more and more television each year.

▪ 5 ▪
THE
PROMOTION
OF
AGGRESSIVE
BEHAVIOR

At the age when education
should start to deal with these impulses
confirmation should not be given
from the outside world
that the same [aggressive] impulses
are upper-most in other people.

Dr. Anna Freud

Stories have always been employed to teach lessons about love, hate, right, wrong, values, and virtue. So strong is the power in stories that Dr. George Gerbner, distinguished professor at the Annenberg School of Communications, says, "If you can control the storytelling of a nation, you don't have to worry about who makes the laws."

Now the new, universal storyteller—television—is beamed directly to the home and to the children there. The storyteller is sanctioned by neither family, nor religion, nor school board. And its easy accessibility has stripped parents of their control.

From the beginning, myth, fairy tale, poetry, and religion have dealt in violence—murder, crucifixion, rape, robbery, guilt, greed, fear, separation. The Greek tragedies feature violence between husband and wife, father and son, parents and children, brothers and sisters. Shakespeare created 116 violent deaths. And traditional fairy tales outdo them all, particularly in violence done to children!

For example, in the tale of *The Three Languages*, the father orders his child killed because he can't learn. Mr. Miacca pinches children first to test their tenderness for eating. In *The Sun, Moon and Talia*, the wife orders her two children killed and serves them as food to their father. Rapunzel is kidnapped. In *The Juniper Tree*, the stepmother feeds the son to his father in a pudding. In *The Three Billy Goats Gruff*, "children" are eaten up ritualistically as the staple in the story line.

Nevertheless, countless people who grew up on scary fairy tales, violent Bible stories, radio thrillers, and comic and film gore are nervous about the generation now growing up on television violence.

TV violence is more dangerous. TV is present in almost all homes and children have unregulated access to it. Not only does the combination of "sight and sound" have particularly potent influence, but TV does not have the built-in protections of print media. To "witness" violence in a book you must be able to read the book. Most children learn to read beginners' books when they are around seven years old. Even this level would not give the child access to unreasonably violent print images: Those stories are written at a reading level that most youngsters would not reach until at least age ten or eleven. Hence, children are protected by their lack of reading skill. If violent stories are read out loud to children, there is another kind of protection: The adult will (presumably) exercise judgment in choosing the story, and the child will "make the pictures" and attach meaning to the words according to his maturity. If the child becomes frightened, at least he is *with somebody*. The reader, perceiving the child's fright, might stop reading or discuss the child's feelings, but in any event the child is not alone.

Violence in film or theater has a "box office barrier." An adult must take the child to the movie house or theater and pay for the ticket before the child has access to the images in the performance. But none of this is so with television. Even the preschool child can experience murder, muggings, rape, and robbery by turning on the TV set in the living room, which any two-year old knows how to do.

Like print, radio operates in the "theater of the mind," where the imagination makes the pictures. Inner pictures offer some protection because they will only be as "bad" as the child's experience will let them be.

But nothing about mass media makes us more uncomfortable than the idea that the quantities of video violence produced in America and consumed around the world might be contributing to the growing epidemic of aggressive behavior. As serious crimes increase and child abuse runs rampant in the United States, and as both children and adults report that they feel fearful of the world, it becomes a logical dream to try to devise ways to control violence as if it were an infectious disease.

For many years people have puzzled over what TV violence does to us. Does it really promote aggression? Is it a cause of crime? How do we know? If there is a relationship, what can we do about it?

Millions of dollars, hundreds of hearings, and repeated research studies have pursued the same basic issue: Does viewing TV violence tend to cause aggressive behavior?

The parade of inquiries, starting in 1954, was led by Senator Estes Kefauver, then chairman of the Senate Subcommittee on Juvenile Delinquency. He concluded that TV contributed to the crime rate.

Senator Thomas Dodd of Connecticut conducted more hearings in 1961 and 1964, in which he protested what he said was the television industry's opportunistic and gratuitous use of violence.

Next came Milton Eisenhower and his National Commission on the Causes and Prevention of Violence, at whose hearings network executives were questioned about research they had promised but had not produced.

Senator John O. Pastore's inquiry in the late sixties and

particularly his questioning of Wilbur H. Stewart, Surgeon General of the Public Health Service, prompted the most major investigation of all. In 1969—with $8 million in funding—the Surgeon General's Committee was established to decide once and for all if viewing TV violence makes youngsters more aggressive. The study, though tarnished by politics and scandal, produced a five-volume *Surgeon General's Scientific Advisory Report on Television and Social Behavior*. Each of the 12 members of the committee, after assessing the research to date, found a relationship between TV violence and aggressive behavior. Their conclusion was unanimous.

The findings were reported broadly on the "entertainment pages" but not on the science or education pages—a put-down for the work of the $8-million committee. Jack Gould, of *The New York Times*, "scooped" the story of the report with an ill-conceived headline, "TV Violence Held Unharmful to Youth." That headline led to years of misunderstanding and misinterpretation of the report itself.

Participants in the Surgeon General's inquiry tell of dissension and politics. John P. Murray, research coordinator, who was present at the deliberation, said: "There was a big move by Government officials to get a consensus report. There was a lot of anger, the meetings were extremely tense with the warring factions sitting at either end of the table, glaring at each other, particularly toward the end."

Soon it became known that the selection of members of the committee had resulted from a procedure in which industry leaders systematically excluded some of the most distinguished researchers on the subject while including a number of network executives. Forty names had been proposed for the 12-person committee, and the television industry had been given the privilege of reviewing the list to make its own recommendations. The industry insisted on the exclusion of Leo Bogart, of the Bureau of Advertising of the American Newspaper Publishers' Association, who had published a book on television; Albert Bandura, psychology professor at Stanford and a foremost expert on children's imitative learning; Leonard Berkowitz, of the University of Wisconsin; and

Leon Eisenberg, chairman of the Department of Psychiatry at Harvard University. The television industry, meantime, was represented by Thomas Coffin, NBC; Joseph Klapper, CBS; and Gerhart D. Weibe, formerly of CBS.

In the summary of their work, more than 100 published papers representing 50 laboratory studies, field studies, and other experiments involving 10,000 children and adolescents from every conceivable background all showed that viewing TV violence makes children more willing to harm others, more aggressive in their play, and more likely to select aggression as the preferred response to conflict situations. In other words, for over a decade it had been clearly demonstrated that children will imitate aggressive acts they watch in film presentations, that repeated viewing of aggressive behavior builds up the probability of aggressive behavior as a conditioned response, and that boys who are heavy viewers of TV violence in childhood tend to be more aggressive adolescents.

Jesse Steinfeld, who was Surgeon General in 1972 when the report was published, said: "There will never be enough research for all the social scientists to agree on . . . but there comes a time when the data are sufficient to justify action. That time has come." But in the decade since the $8-million report virtually nothing has been done.

To supplement the experts' opinions and observations, there are now numerous scientifically conducted research projects in the form of content analyses of TV programs, clinical research on specific behaviors, longitudinal studies on child development over many years, and some "projective" experiments in which children draw or talk about their feelings, fantasies, or inner pictures. What are the facts about the effects of TV violence on children?

AGGRESSION AS PART OF LIFE

To begin with, we know that aggression is part of life. All babies are born with it but do not know what to do with it until they're taught. What comes with each human being as a natural characteristic will turn into either useful assertiveness toward positive ends or raw aggressiveness of a destructive, violent kind.

Children harness native aggression and use it to play, to learn, to dream, to care, to compete, to work. Although aggression is a fact of life, violent destructiveness is not a part of all human life. Certain other advanced Western countries, such as Britain, show much less aggressive behavior than the United States; the annual number of murders in the whole British Isles is less than that in New York City. In some fashion or other, human behavior is what people learn, and in some countries we learn to be violently destructive whereas in others we do not. As the song from *South Pacific* points out, a child has to be carefully taught at an early age to love *and* to hate.

At the national hearings on violence conducted by the Parent–Teachers Association (PTA) in 1978, psychiatrists pointed out that human life cannot be divorced from conflict. "Conflict is a part of every human situation," said Dr. Roderick Gorney, professor of psychiatry at the University of California. "But conflict does not have to involve destructive violence. In most human situations conflict is resolved without destructive violence."

KIDS SEE EXCESSIVE VIDEO VIOLENCE

Another fact to be confronted is the huge amount of time children spend watching television violence. By age five, the typical child in the United States has logged over 200 hours of violent images, and the average fourteen-year-old has witnessed the killing of 13,000 human beings—usually without pain, funeral, or grieving relatives.

Although definitions and coding procedures differ, regular reports on violent content appearing over the last 20 years show a clear pattern of escalating levels of aggression through the 1950's and 1960's. The all-time high was reported in 1967 when 80 to 90 percent of all programs contained violence.[1]

Not only do news, sports, police shows, and action-adventure series all show people slug-punch-pounding their way through life, but standard *children's cartoons* are the most violent programs of all! Studies in the late 1960's showed six times more violence (and two times as much advertising) in Saturday morning children's programming as in adult prime time. In the fall of 1978, after more than a decade of public concern about violence, the rate of violent incidents on weekend network children's programming actually rose to a near-record level of 25 incidents per hour, according to Dr. Nancy Signorielli of the Annenberg School of Communications at the University of Pennsylvania.

Cartoon violence does not represent a form of "artistic conflict." It is carefully and deliberately used to play on the child's vulnerabilities, to get him or her to watch, and to lure the largest possible audience for the purpose of selling products. Violent cartoons provide the easiest means of attracting the entire two-to-eleven age group and therefore, according to advertisers, are the best places to "hang a commercial."

Joseph Barbera, of the Hanna-Barbera animation studio in California, has said that his studio manufactures lots of violence for children because "all they [networks] want is out-of-this-world hard action."[2]

Some cartoons are superviolent. The National Association for Better Broadcasting (NABB) in California conducted an image-by-image content analysis of the cartoon stock and sorted out 140 shows that it deemed "excessively violent," such as *Groovie Goolies*, which features monsters, noise, ridicule, explosions, and torture-for-fun; *The Munsters*, which focuses on Grandpa, who is a vampire; and *Batman*, the most popular socko-entertainment; as well as *Aquaman, Birdman, Superman, Spiderman, Gigantor, Eight Man, Marine Boy, Shazam, Speed Racer*, and scores more.

In addition to daytime cartoons, children see considerable violence in such evening programs as *Emergency, Six Million Dollar Man, The Incredible Hulk, Nancy Drew, The Hardy Boys*, news, and police shows. Los Angeles station KTLA even rescheduled *Starsky and Hutch*, an excessively violent program, at 6 P.M., when there is known to be a large audience of young children.

Some of the most hurtful violence, including episodes of wife-beating, child abuse, and drug use, appears before millions of children in the form of program promotions aired during children's typical viewing hours. "Stay up," the child is told during a four o'clock show, "and watch Barretta sink into the world of drugs." That promo was followed by another for *Charlie's Angels*, a late-night show known for its sexual suggestiveness. One parent wrote to a consumer organization: "Last night at 8:15 my children and I saw an NBC promotional ad for *Police Woman*, which is a program aired at 10 P.M. The ad showed a man beating up his wife while a small child looked on from the crib. Angry shouting and screaming accompanied the beating."

Children in other countries consume a great deal of our American-made TV violence, partly because it is usually cheaper to buy or "rent" American fare in syndication than to pay local production costs.

What will happen in the 1980's as certain trends materialize—more and more multiple-set households, cable TV with dozens of channels per set, giant-sized screens—and competition for audience continues? Will tomorrow's local cable stations, like today's broadcasters in developing countries, use the cheapest programs available just to fill up empty channels, just to do business?

CHILDREN ATTRACTED TO VIOLENCE

Children seem to like violence. They are attracted to it. Seven-year-old John would choose *Batman* instead of *Mister Rogers'*. An eight-year-old said to his mother, "I'd like to see a war." "Do you mean really be there?" asked the mother. "Yes, but if they asked, I'd say I'm a sightseer."

The fascination with aggression is innate, numerous psychiatrists point out. Dr. Anna Freud has described the psychological reasons for children's fascination with aggressiveness and why seeing aggressive displays routinely may be injurious to the small child's development. She and Dorothy Burlingham pointed out in their book *War and Children* that it is part of the

education of the young child to learn to deal with his natural
aggressiveness. The urge to hurt and destroy must be suppressed and eventually redirected to "fight the difficulties of
the outer world"—toward healthy competition and worthwhile accomplishments. While a child is learning to deal with
his aggressive tendencies, it can be harmful for him to be
exposed to violence and aggression in others. Such exposure
provides him with "confirmation . . . that the same impulses
are uppermost in other people" and could subvert his own
struggle to overcome them. In her work with children of war,
Anna Freud learned of the need for protecting them from more
than physical harm. She observed:

> Children will play joyfully on bombed sites and around
> bomb craters, they will play with blasted bits of furniture
> and throw bricks from crumbled walls at each other. But it
> becomes impossible to educate them towards a repression
> of and reaction against destruction while they are doing
> so. . . . Children have to be safeguarded against the primi-
> tive horrors of the war, not because horrors and atrocities
> are so strange to them, but because we want them at this
> decisive stage of their development to overcome and
> estrange themselves from the primitive and atrocious
> wishes of their own infantile nature.[3]

While young children may be attracted to violence, they
cannot necessarily sort out the experience or differentiate their
inner world from the outer world. Similarly, young children
do not differentiate fantasy from reality. Although children
may verbalize adult edicts and prescriptions, they do not
perceive or reason like adults; in fact, their lives are not ruled
by reason at all but by their powerful *feelings* and animistic
thinking (see Chapter 3, "The Effects on Learning and Perception"). For the child of six and under, dreams are real.
Television is real.

Certain kinds of "fantasy violence," such as performed by
the Bionic Woman and Six Million Dollar Man become "real"
for the very young TV child. These "reconstituted" human
beings, with superhuman powers, are routinely solving impos-

sible situations. These images may increase the six-year-old's feelings of helplessness, which he is struggling so hard to overcome in real-life childhood.

The mother of a five-year-old and an eight-year-old observed: "When the children see 'bionic violence' they are doubly frightened. Run-of-the-mill violence might be understood. The older child might even imagine that if someone punches you, you could hit 'em back. But it is impossible for a child to imagine removing a bomb from under a river or rescuing someone from a fire in her space capsule. It's too much for the child."

KIDS COPY TV VIOLENCE

Most behaviors are acquired through imitation or observational learning, and some violent behavior may be copied from television. Examples of crimes copied from TV have included a nine-year-old's effort to slip his teacher a box of poisoned chocolates, a seven-year-old's use of ground glass in the family stew, a seventeen-year-old's re-enactment of a televised rape and murder by bludgeoning the victim's head and slashing her throat, and a fifteen-year-old's real-life rerun of a rape with a broomstick televised in the movie *Born Innocent*. The legal argument in a Florida murder case hinged on the argument that the teen-age murderer "couldn't help it" because he was under the influence of television. Whenever the film *Doomsday Flight*, a film demonstrating how to hijack a plane, is shown, actual hijackings increase dramatically. A study of 100 juvenile offenders commissioned by ABC found that no fewer than 22 confessed to having copied criminal techniques from television.

Professor Albert Bandura of Stanford University pioneered research on the imitation of televised behavior by children. Bandura, in addition to his reputation as a highly respected social scientist, has the distinction of having been excluded by TV executives when it was proposed in 1969 that he be part of the Surgeon General's Committee.

In general, his work shows that children who view TV

become involved in three processes. First, they are exposed to new behaviors and characters, then they learn to do or acquire those behaviors, and eventually they accept them as their own.

Typical of Bandura's experiments on "observational learning" is one involving 96 nursery school children, ages three to five, which aimed to discover whether prior exposure to adult aggression would influence a child's reaction to being frustrated. In the experiment, one-fourth of the children were randomly assigned to an experimental condition in which they were taken into a room to play with a variety of toys including a 5-foot inflated doll that was weighted at the bottom. Soon an adult began hitting the "Bobo" doll repeatedly with a mallet, employing distinctive and dramatic techniques that would be new to the children who were watching. The second group of children was put in an identical play environment but shown a film of the adult hitting the doll. A third group saw an animated film presentation of the doll being hit by an adult in a cat costume. The fourth group, the control group, saw no form of the beating at all.

After the viewing period, each child was taken to another room filled with highly attractive toys and invited to play with them. But as soon as the children began to play, the experimenter interrupted them, saying that she had decided to save these toys for some other children, and then took the children to another room in which there were some very ordinary toys together with a Bobo doll and a mallet such as most of the children had seen earlier. Each child was observed for 20 minutes through a one-way glass to see how he or she would react to the frustrating turn of events.

When the total of aggressive responses was calculated it showed that prior exposure to the adult aggressive example had a marked effect on the children's response. Children in the control group, who had not seen the adult hitting the doll, received an average aggression score of 54; children who had watched the live model received 82; those who saw the real person in a film received 92; children who saw the cartoon version received the highest score of 99.[4] (Researchers will still query: Why was the *animated cat* more readily imitated in

Bandura's study? Do children perceive animals in storybooks and TV as part of reality or as part of fantasy? Do they perceive animation as "more real" or "less real" than other kinds of programming? Do they model themselves after animals more easily than after human figures? In addition to observing the long-time popularity of animals in fables, fairy tales, and nursery rhymes, widely used projective tests such as the Rorschach and the Children's Apperception Test (C.A.T.) indicate that children have a strong identification with animals. This is particularly so for small or immature children up to ten years of age.)

In contrast to Bandura's work, however, one school of thought minimizes the link between TV violence and observational behavior. Proponents of the "catharsis" theory hold that by watching violence on TV the viewer can release aggressive impulses vicariously without actually harming anyone, thus reducing the need to be violent.

Research does not bear out this theory, however. Most studies point to an increase rather than a decrease of aggressiveness following the viewing of violence. The Surgeon General's Committee, after reviewing the relevant research, found "no evidence that would support a catharsis interpretation."[5]

The bulk of research supports the disturbing observation that viewing TV violence makes children more aggressive in their play and more willing to use violent behaviors as a means to solve personal problems. The lesson of TV is that violence works. Heavy viewers, significantly more than light viewers, have the attitude that violence is an effective method for solving their personal problems. Dr. George Gerbner and Dr. Larry Gross conducted sets of surveys of children who were "heavy viewers" or "light viewers." They asked: "How often is it all right to hit someone if you are mad at them?" They found that heavy viewers of television, more often than light viewers, respond that it is "almost always right" to hit someone.

Hundreds of similar studies have shown that viewing TV violence produces increased aggressive behavior in the young, according to data in the Surgeon General's Report. Children are just as happy to imitate villains as heroes. They will copy verbal assault as well as physical aggressions and will imitate both live-action figures and cartoon characters.

Most of the research on TV and aggressive behaviors is in the form of laboratory or field studies that can comment mainly on the immediate or transient effects of viewing TV violence but have little to say about how TV might interact with personality factors. Longitudinal studies can add insight.

A 20-year longitudinal study in the sixties and seventies in upstate New York by Monroe M. Lefkowitz and his colleagues charted possible predictors of aggressive behavior—including television—and checked them out in a sample of third-graders, who were retested after the 12th grade. The researchers *found a clear correlation between the amount of TV violence viewed by eight-year-old boys and subsequent aggressiveness in young adulthood.* The study showed that the more violent the programs watched by boys in third grade, the more aggressive was their behavior both at that time and ten years later. This research also clearly associated high mobility of families and the development of aggressive behaviors. Lefkowitz and others report on many variables, including peer-related aggression, father's occupational status, child's IQ, father's aggressiveness, mother's aggressiveness, parents' punishment of the child, amount and nature of television watched, etc. The authors conclude that "close communication with one's child has both immediate and long-term effects in reducing aggression."[6]

It should be noted that while Lefkowitz accounts clearly for the relationship between TV viewing at age eight and aggressive behavior at least through adolescence, some people will claim that these eight-year-olds had a pattern of watching TV violence because of hormonal factors and that their biological makeup accounts for both their TV choices at eight and their later aggressiveness.

Violence on TV is sometimes defended by those who think that the conventional accompanying message "crime does not pay" justifies the highly visual fistfight complete with knives and blood. Although the child viewer may be told "crime does not pay," what he remembers is the glamour of the fistfight.

The reason for this is that the fighting is in the visual portion, and the contextual message is in the audio. Dr. Aimee Dorr of the University of Southern California investigated the responses to TV of children under six. She reported:

> Young children are apparently learning from television that aggression is a good strategy or at least an exceedingly common one. They are not learning the contextual message that crime doesn't pay or that alternatives to aggression are desirable. When children are given a mixed message about the context for aggression on television, they come away believing simply that the more aggression they see, the more they should aggress. This is especially true for young children.[7]

TEACHERS' EXPERIENCE

Anecdotal evidence in quantity can be as valuable as formal research. Schoolteachers who have taught for 10 or 15 years are among the best observers of trends and unusual behaviors. Teachers across the country are giving similar reports about TV's disruptive effects on classroom behavior. For example, at the Horace Mann School for Nursery Years in New York City, teachers report such behavior as:

- Children describing films they had seen, such as *The Towering Inferno, Earthquake,* and *The Godfather.*
- The interruption of peaceful block-building sessions by cries of "earthquake" and demolitions of constructions.
- Recurrent choruses of "I'm Batman, I'm Superman, I'm a monster, pow, pow, chop, chop," to the occasional accompaniment of wrestling or karate chops.

Whether or not a particular child watches TV at home, the mass culture, aggressive behaviors, video values, and loud language all get recycled on the school playground. "Oh, yeah? . . . So? . . . Who cares? . . . Dummy! . . . Dingbat! . . ."

Watching TV violence can even alter a child's fundamental attitudes. Television promotes fear. In a glamorized and overstated way the world is shown on TV to be a dangerous place, notes Dr. George Gerbner. He says: "There is a consistent relationship between fear and the amount of television watched. They [heavy watchers] do perceive the world as much more violent, and they are much more fearful."

"The fear that somebody bad might get into the house is so widespread, cutting across all residential, economic and ethnic groups, that the influence of television is certainly suggested," says a report of a national survey of children by the Foundation for Child Development in New York. But there is more direct evidence in this survey linking television to children's fears. "Just under a quarter of the children said they feel afraid of TV programs where people fight and shoot guns! And children who are reported to be heavy TV watchers—whose parents say they watch four or more hours of television on the average weekday—were twice as likely as other children to report that they 'get scared often.'"

DESENSITIZATION

Desensitization is perhaps the most serious effect of all of widespread TV violence. Psychologists say that the TV child develops a thick-skinned detachment, a cynical outlook. Constantly exposed to the bloody punch or push, the noise, and the rough language of TV, children learn to accept violence. What is amazing and shameful is the ease with which people accept violence as being not only possible, but probable and "OK." We learn to watch brutalities on the TV news without responding and to see them in the streets without responding.

It is likely that we have been conditioned by TV viewing itself not to respond as well as by habituation to the violent programs. Dr. Erik Peper has said: "The horror of television is that the information goes in, but we don't react to it until later when we don't know what we're reacting to. When you watch television you are training yourself not to react and so, later on, you're doing things without knowing why you're doing them or where they came from." With desensitization, there is no outrage over destructive aggression. Like some spiritual or

emotional novocaine that dulls painful feelings, desensitization limits conscious emotions to only those that may be joyful
or delicate in spirit.

There are many kinds of violence aside from the physical
that play into this pattern of desensitization. Verbal violence,
perceptual violence, and emotional violence are all by-prod-
ucts of the TV-viewing experience. Threats and insults are
forms of verbal violence. TV puts pressure on the human
being's perceptual apparatus via noise levels and the overload
of visual stimuli. The picture changes roughly every six
seconds on commercial TV—violent jolts per minute to the
immature sensory system. Emotional violence has to do with
all that strikes at a human being's dignity or worth. Television
is full of it. This includes racism, sexism, age-ism, and neglect,
as discussed in Chapter 7, "The Effects on Social Relationships."

Parents admit wearily that they cannot provide all the
protection needed. One made the case for broadcaster responsibility this way: What if you looked out the window and saw a
vicious, drunken gang running through the streets brandishing
handguns and knives and yelling wildly? With concern for the
youngsters who play in the neighborhood, you call the police
and say, "There are outlaws running through the streets!
Won't you do something?" But the officer says, "Well, lady,
they're your kids—you'll have to go out there and protect
them." Helplessly, we realize the impossibility of tagging
along with a child all day to guard against the possibility of
dangerous situations.

It is with respect for the limits of the parental role and the
complexity of the media-saturated society that citizens have
organized to create standards and policy structures to govern
the flow of violence through the public airwaves. Societal
progress is reported in Chapter 10, "Public Action."

■ 6 ■
THE
EFFECTS
ON
HEALTH
AND
LIFE-STYLE

Can the promotion of frivolous, wasteful
food products be condoned in a world
rapidly outrunning its food supply?
Can we afford to let television
make our children just like us—
the world's greediest consumers?

Joan Gussow, Chairperson
Department of Nutrition
Columbia Teachers College

Millions of young children are demonstrating in the supermarkets of America. They campaign in the aisles, running up
and down singing TV jingles and repeating TV product names.
They pass up healthy foods but tug on Mama's pocketbook for
one more package of Froot Loops, Freakies, Pop Tarts, or Ring
Dings. An advertising executive for Oscar Meyer and Co. once
explained, "When you sell a kid on your product, if he can't
get it, he will throw himself on the floor, stamp his feet and
cry. You can't get a reaction like that out of an adult."[1]

Knowing children's vulnerabilities, advertisers spend about $700 million yearly pitching products at them. Advertising strategists know from their sophisticated research that children will learn efficiently from television and will easily become the advertiser's representative in the home. *The typical child in America sees roughly 400 TV advertisements a week* that tell him what to like, what to want, what to do, and what to beg for. Long before the TV child can make purchases by himself, he will influence the consuming behavior of adults.

THE PROOF IS IN THE PROFITS

In the 1960's TV advertisers discovered how "efficient" it is to sell certain kinds of products to certain kinds of people— radial tires to men, floor wax to women, candy to kids. Ad experts explained that it would be a mistake to advertise products intended for women in a program with mostly male viewers. This know-how helped to promote what became known as the "youth market," in which children became prime targets for junk food and toys. Les Brown of *The New York Times* has written:

> . . . a number of factors converged around 1965 to make children's programs a major profit center of networks: first, the proliferation of multi-set households, which broke up family viewing and loosened the child's control over the program his or her parents would watch; second, the drift to participation advertising as opposed to full sponsorships, which encouraged more advertisers to use the medium; and third, the discovery that a relatively "pure" audience of children could be corralled on Saturday mornings (and to a lesser extent on Sundays) where air time was cheaper, advertising quotas were wide open and children could be reached by the devices used years before by the comic books.[2]

Until the mid-1970's the broadcasters' code permitted 16 minutes of nonprogram material (ads and promos) per hour in weekend children's television but only 9.5 minutes in adult prime-time programming.

By the late 1960's child advocate groups began to question the morality of advertising to children. The chief group, Action for Children's Television (ACT), contends that all advertising aimed at children is inherently deceptive because no small child has the judgment to stand up against an American advertising agency. Advertising to children is "like shooting fish in a barrel," said Joan Cooney, developer of Sesame Street.

ADVERTISING CONTENT

Kids know about Crest and fluoride before they have a full set of teeth. "Brush your teeth" and "Drink milk" are messages delivered by TV commercials, and while such encouragements may be supportive of a health goal, a closer look at advertising shows that health/nutrition ads are indeed rare. What the typical child *does see* is 400 commercials a week—a fast-moving mural of ads for Secret, Raid, Dawn, Dash, Brut, Ban, Leggs, Lego, Freakies, Frankenberry, Froot Loops, and so on.

Junk foods head the list of products promoted by commercials on children's TV. Over 50 percent of the ads in children's programming are for food, primarily sugar-coated cereals, cookies, candies, and soft drinks. Thirty percent are for toys and (between 1965 and 1975) 10 percent were for vitamin pills.[3] (Vitamin pills were pushed on children's TV until ACT held a spotlight on the practice. The sellers of the novelty-form, candylike pills used hero figures such as Spiderman to induce children to ask for and consume the pills. In the ads Spiderman talked about "delicious, chewable" vitamins and "new superhero vitamins." While this advertising practice was carried out, numerous children were reported hospitalized for overdoses of vitamins.) Peggy Charren of ACT points out: "Almost all the TV ads targeted to children are for toys and junk food. We've found that most of the food advertising is for products children don't have to eat—nonnutritive, cavity-causing foods. Companies are designing foods that would never be on the market if it weren't for television and its ability to sell to children. They actually design highly sugared cereals like Frankenberry and Cocoa Pebbles and Cookie Crisps because they can push them to kids on television."

When a New York State watchdog committee monitored nine months of TV fare, their study showed that the most frequent commercials were for cereals (3,832), followed by candy and gum (1,627) and then cookies and crackers, noncarbonated "fruit" drinks, spaghetti and macaroni, cakes, pies, pastry, desserts, citrus, carbonated soda pop, ice cream, soups, etc. In nine months of study, the researchers found only one commercial for vegetables, one for cheese, and none for milk, butter, eggs, or vegetable juices.

There are certain brand names that every child knows because they are advertised relentlessly on television: Milky Way, Baby Ruth, Butterfingers, Mr. Goodbar, Junior Mints, M & M's, Pop Tarts, Devil Dogs, Ring Dings, Yankee Doodles, Yodels, Oreos, Big Wheels, Twinkies, Sugar Wafers, Charm Big Tops, Milk Duds, Tootsie Pops, Tootsie Rolls, Turkish Taffy, and so on.

Toys are the number-two item advertised on children's television. Colorful, mechanical, plastic, high-priced, and designed to "show well," action toys with moving parts look nice on TV. Notice the bikes, cycles, and skateboards zooming downhill or careening around corners. But a teddy bear looks dead on TV—therefore it is not a "good" TV toy.

During the Christmas season, the only period when toys are pushed more than junk food, the commercials tend to be for superhero dolls and other paraphernalia of the TV culture. The current toy assemblage includes superheroes (Spiderman and Wonder Woman), singers (Donnie and Marie), athletes (Muhammed Ali), actresses (Farrah Fawcett), and famous monsters (Godzilla). Each holiday season has its favorites: According to ACT's newsmagazine, re: act, 1978 was to be the Star Wars Christmas. Kenner Toys' aggressive advertising practices gave it the edge in winning an exclusive worldwide rights agreement to market Star Wars models. Sales success

with the Six Million Dollar Man and Bionic Woman convinced
Twentieth Century Fox to sign with Kenner. TV-licensed
action figures had already helped Kenner increase its sales
from $78 million in 1973 to $138 million in 1976, and Kenner
predicted that the *Star Wars* license would push the company's sales to well over $250 million. Just some of the
offerings available in this TV-toy avalanche include the following: 12 two-to four-inch-high *Star Wars* action figures
($1.99 each); the *Star Wars* Land Speeder ($5.99); the *Star
Wars* Death Star Space Station ($17.87); the eleven-and-a-half
inch Large Luke Skywalker and Large Princess Leia Organa
($8.99 each); the *Star Wars* Radio Control R2-D2 ($29.99); the
Star Wars Laser Rifle ($12.99); the *Star Wars* Electronic Battle
Game ($34.88).[4] The science fiction market promises to remain
strong through 1980 when the *Star Wars* sequel is released.

   The typical American family will dole out $95 per year per
child for toys, and 70 percent of that is spent during the
holiday season. Most major toy purchases are made in the
weeks before Christmas, so pressure is on the toymakers to sell
aggressively during that season. A vice-president of a large toy
company with an $8-million advertising budget explains, "We
have an economic need to 'showcase' and demonstrate our
toys to a mass audience of children." He recalls:

> I can remember when Teddy Bears and Shirley Temple
> dolls were our big sellers. . . . In those days stores had
> long glass counters—you could see things close up, touch
> them, wind them up and see how they ran across the floor.
> And at Christmastime New York's department stores
> would hire extra people to be "demonstrators" to show off
> the toys and tell customers how to use them. That's how
> customers decided what to buy. Today the demonstrators
> and the long glass counters are largely gone, and toys
> come to stores in sealed boxes. But kids will have seen the
> toys on TV.[5]

When a manufacturer buys advertising time on TV it boosts
the price of the toy. A toy dealer in Berkeley, California, said,
"A sponge rubber ball, that would sell 'plain' for 29–39 cents,

but packaged and advertised the retail price is $1.29!" He also remarked that television toy commercials have created "giant toy manufacturers who stifle competition and force stores to take unwanted merchandise."

In addition to the price and the ad pitches, parents object to the *toys themselves*. What kind of values or behavior do they encourage? What kinds of play do they suggest? As discussed in Chapter 3, "The Effects on Learning and Perception," television toys are too often highly structured and tend to limit imaginative, creative play.

TECHNIQUES

Fast cuts, camera angles, laugh tracks, animation, disclaimers, and premiums all have hidden persuasions that children (and adults) do not decipher. Calvin Collier, former FTC chairman, points out:

> When advertising itself is addressed to a special audience, such as children, we must view it through a double prism. Not only must we consider established standards of legality but we also have to take into account the special needs of the child audience. It is axiomatic that an advertisement which would not break the law when beamed to an adult audience . . . may well be deceptive or unfair when it is beamed at children.

Children see and perceive in a way that is different from adults. What an adult perceives as "true" may not be perceived as "true" by a child. Because of this, child advocates say that advertising should be held to standards of fairness that would require broadcast messages to be "true to the child's perceptions." If the dynamite in that phrase could be spelled out and translated into advertising regulations, the reforms in advertising techniques would be vast. Many of the current production techniques would be called into question. These techniques include the following:

- Loud, brightly colored, action-oriented segments, sometimes a few decibels louder than the program. Knowing that bright colors attract attention, some cereals are designed for the color factor. Froot Loops look prettier on TV than oatmeal!
- Integration of ads into the program as much as possible so that the program and the commercial are not clearly separated. Most young children do not differentiate between the program and the ad and therefore do not know when somebody is trying to sell them something. For this reason, the Federal Communications Commission has considered regulation that would require "a separating device" via either the audio or video portion, such as "face to black" before the start of the commercial, or the clustering of ads at the end of the program.
- Frequent repetition of very short segments, which plays to the short attention span of the child. (Repetition works!)
- Three-camera production, standard in commercial production, which allows for unusual angles in succession and quick cuts that demand quick shifts in vision. These techniques are alien to the child's normal way of seeing and do violence to the immature perceptual apparatus.
- Laugh track and noise track underscoring visual and auditory messages. The laugh track is an effective tool used to attract children's attention and tell them what's funny or pleasing.
- Animation, which is appealing to children.
- Outright deceptions or tricks employed to make products look irresistible on TV. The FTC questioned the use of certain "studio methods" used in "demonstration" ads. For example, it challenged whether it was proper, in filming a commercial for Campbells Soup, to put clear glass marbles in the soup to make the vegetables cluster near the surface.

NAGGING FOR PRODUCTS

The effects of viewing 400 commercials a week are changing children's expectations, attitudes, nutrition, play, and even their relationships with their parents. Children want and beg for whatever products are advertised on television. After all, it's the goal of the ad to make kids want things badly enough that the parent buys them. Mothers complain about children seeing ads for things that are obviously nonessential and nonnutritious. The barrage of requests is tiring, but nagging works. Mothers give in to nagging (by kids five to seven years old) for TV cereals about 88 percent of the time, according to a study by the Harvard Business School. The study showed, in addition, that mothers yield to requests for snack food 52 percent of the time; candy, 40 percent; and soft drinks, 38 percent.

Via TV the child becomes the advertiser's representative in the home, and, although children do not purchase products themselves, they control a large percentage of the dollar for certain products. Children tend to trust and believe television indiscriminately, giving the advertising message the nuance of an "order" rather than an "invitation" to buy the product.

In interviews with mothers in Denver, Colorado, most agreed that the toy manufacturers make Christmastime unbearable for them. One mother said that commercials "give children a purchasing power they shouldn't have. Many times they make me feel guilty." Another mother felt: "It creates a *need*. If a child has a genuine interest in something, that's fine, but if it's *created*, something they really don't want, it's not good." Mothers agreed that there's a sort of "keeping up with the Joneses" produced by toy commercials.

Nagging for TV products ultimately injures the parent–child relationship. Even before the influence of television many mothers have grown weary with the day-in day-out duties of the parent-in-charge, sometimes complaining of the "negative function" inevitably involved. The parent who is home with the kids all day will have to exercise judgment to say "no" to the baby who chews on the electrical cord, and "no" to touching the stove, and "no" to the toddler about to run into the street; to intervene in sibling battles, and to be firm about naptime. To be consistent about discipline is a tiring though necessary activity. Mothers complain about their "negative function" in carrying out normal parental behavior. They often feel that "daddy coming home" at the end of the day is all fun and games and that the burdensome and negative part of child rearing is laid on the mothers.

Having to say "no" to incessant TV-produced requests adds to the negative function of the mother. In exasperation, one parent cried out: "How many times should I be expected to say 'no' for products that aren't good for my child?" In one survey, numerous mothers said that the commercials tend to start arguments in the family, especially during the holiday season. One said: "It should be done in good taste. The sponsors don't have to push it at you. If commercials are necessary, they should be true. They have a tendency to grossly exaggerate the value of the product."

Parents' unrest with commercials is increased by their distaste for the products themselves. Too many of the toys are expensive, most are intricate and break easily, and they are frequently so glamorized on TV that the child does not even recognize the toy when the package is opened.

NUTRITION AND LEARNING ABILITY

Obviously, the child's nutrition and eating habits are affected by TV, and these in turn govern physical health, intelligence, and learning behaviors. Millions of children and adults suffer from dental caries (cavities), obesity, hyperactivity, and hypertension—all caused or aggravated by the "modern American diet."

When U.S. agricultural capabilities expanded after World War II, a revolution in food processing took place. Now, whenever we walk into a supermarket, we must choose from the incredible variety and abundance of available foods. But our ability to choose well has not increased with the food supply.

During the last 20 years the consumption of dairy products has declined 21 percent, while the consumption of sugar has gone sky-high. Soft-drink consumption rose 80 percent, that of pies, cookies, and desserts went up 70 percent, and snacks are up by 85 percent.[6]

Television makes children more familiar with sugar products than with other kinds of food, and this familiarity tells them what to look for or see in the supermarket. On Saturday morning cartoons a child will watch about 20 ads per hour. Seventy-five percent of these may be for sugary snack foods— Tootsie Pops, Ring Dings, Sugar Smacks, and the like.

The high-sugar diet recommended by TV advertising has been shown to have ill effects on the health of the young (and old). Yet the typical American consumes 28 teaspoons of sugar a day! A lot of this sugar is masked in foods that we might not think of as sugar foods. Which food do you think contains a greater percentage of sugar: Heinz Tomato Ketchup or Sealtest Chocolate Ice Cream? Wishbone Russian Dressing or Coca-Cola? Coffee-Mate Non-Dairy Creamer or a bar of Hershey's Milk Chocolate? *Consumer Reports* found that the Heinz Ketchup is 29 percent sugar, compared with 21 percent for the ice cream. If you put Wishbone Russian dressing on a salad, you're pouring 30 percent sugar, a proportion more than three times that of Coke. The Coffee-Mate, which is supposed to be a substitute for cream, contains 65 percent sugar, against 51 percent for a Hershey bar. If you prepare your chicken with Shake 'N Bake Barbeque Style, you're getting a coating that's 51 percent sugar. A bowl of Quaker 100% Natural Cereal gives you 24 percent sugar.[7]

These kinds of processed foods—high in sugar and low in protein—are sold to the public every day on television. "It's a health hazard in the living room," says Dr. Richard Feinbloom, a family doctor from Cambridge, Massachusetts, who testified before the FTC hearings on advertising aimed at children in 1979.

It is well known that a high-sugar/low-protein diet is apt to have ill effects on the health of the young. Cavities are caused by sugar. The consensus of research and expert opinion is that sugar, consumed several times a day, is the substance most likely to cause tooth decay. Ninety-eight percent of the nation's children suffer from tooth decay, and the average American adult has 18 decayed, missing, or filled teeth.

The diet in most primitive populations contains very little sugar (and no refined sugar). Upon exposure to a "modern" diet with its substantial amount of refined sugar, the number of decayed teeth in these populations has been shown to increase dramatically. This kind of study has been done with Eskimos and tribes in Africa and South America.

A famous study in a Swedish mental institution clearly demonstrated that two other factors are crucial in determining the severity of decay: the form in which the sugar was presented and the time of day at which the sugar was eaten. Those patients consuming between-meal snacks showed more caries than those consuming the same amount of sugar at meals. Also, forms of sweets likely to stick to the teeth— caramel candy bars, cookies, sticky pastries, sucking candy, soda pop, all of which contain a high percentage of sugar, chiefly sucrose—were shown consistently to be the greatest producers of caries. Soft drinks also contain quite a dose of caffein, a natural substance which is known to cause anxiety reactions and sleeplessness.[8] Why is it that advertisers feel that they should take caffein out of their own coffee for health reasons yet put it back in their children's soda pop?

Tests have shown that intelligence can be affected by the adequacy of the mother's diet before conception, during pregnancy, and during the early years of life. Poor diets affect intellectual development as much as they affect physical development. In humans, as well as other animals, rapid brain development during the first three months after conception depends largely on the metabolism of protein. Deficiencies of high-quality protein can cause retardation; the harm can never be undone. Stomachs that are filled with "empty calories" have no space left for the protein foods that are available—a phenomenon that has been called the "malnutrition of afflu-ence."

In recent years, teen-age pregnancies have risen dramatically and teen-agers are apt to be junk food addicts, weaned on years of TV junk food advertising.

OBESITY AS A NATIONAL HEALTH PROBLEM

Obesity is a disease that now affects about one-third of American children. Although obesity isn't hereditary, it does run in families because they share eating habits, menus, and diets. Theories of disease are beginning to include nutrition as an important factor. Six of the ten leading causes of death in the United States—heart disease, stroke, cancer, diabetes, artereosclerosis, and cirrhosis of the liver—have been connected to diet. Most of these conditions are related to two major nutritional factors: obesity and excessive intake of fat and sugar. Children can become habituated and addicted to sugar and fatty foods. Their childhood nutrition habits lay the groundwork for adult health or disease patterns. Unfortunately, the sugary, fatty foodstuffs that promote disease patterns are exactly the products pushed incessantly on TV aimed at children.

In addition to physical condition, moods and activity levels may be affected by blood sugar and the presence of food additives in the system. Hyperactivity has been on the increase in elementary schools and now stands as a diagnosed condition in anywhere from 4 to 20 percent of the child population. Dr. B. F. Feingold of the Kaiser–Permanente Medical Center in San Francisco attributes hyperactivity in the children he studied to the increase in chemical additives in the diet and cites parallel graphs which show the incidence of the disease and the dollar value of soft drinks and synthetic flavors sold in the past ten years. In controlled studies, Dr. Feingold has been able to reduce levels of hyperactivity by controlling diet, specifically by eliminating processed foods which are high in sugar, food flavors, and colors.[9]

When considering the known relationship between life-style and health, it is shocking to realize that our enlightened population of adults (which spends millions on diet books, health foods, and jogging apparatus) will permit the worst foods available to be aggressively sold to the young, whom they allow to sit passively munching snack foods and watching hundreds of TV commercials a week. It is a peculiar form of child abuse.

CONSUMPTION AS A LIFE-STYLE

The most serious effects, however, of seeing hundreds of commercials each week is that they teach children a life-style of consumption. Children learn the "material-goods-make-happiness" ethic very early. Watching this "corporate mural," a viewer sees that every problem can be solved by a product— in just 30 seconds.

In spite of inflation, frenetic consumption increases. Lots of people sense that it's crazy, even while they participate in consuming TV food, toys, gadgets, cars, and more TV programs. A mother of young children says, "I have the feeling that I should buy more presents just to fill up the space under the tree." A first-grade teacher says that the children she sees in school tend to take things for granted. "When Jimmy's calculator disappeared—apparently stolen—he didn't hunt for it or even feel too badly. 'It doesn't matter, my mother will buy another one,' he said."

Concern of many people is sharpened by awareness of larger trends. Nutritionist Joan Gussow says: "If we are—and we are—coming into a time when austerity and not affluence, when self-restraint and not self-indulgence, and sense and not sensation must dictate some of our consuming behavior . . . what on earth do we do about those commercial messages 'acquire, acquire, acquire, buy, buy, buy, indulge, indulge, indulge' which the television set beams to our children?" [10]

CYNICISM ABOUT ADS AND INSTITUTIONS

Eventually the accumulation of TV commercials makes children cynical if no less vulnerable. By the time a child is eleven or twelve, he or she is likely to believe that TV commercials are "all lies"—that's what most kids told researchers in a study commissioned and reported by the *Harvard Business Review* in 1975. The researchers learned that children of age five or six tend to swallow the commercial "whole." For this-age child the commercial is like pure information. However, the study indicated that by the time the child is eleven or twelve, he decides that all advertising is a sham. By then the child has consumed thousands of ads, seen plastic toys that break on Christmas morning, and knows that junk foods really aren't good for you. But children buy them anyway, even as they generalize that if ads "lie" then the ad writers are lying; that, in fact, adults lie and institutions lie. "By eleven . . . most children have already become cynical—ready to believe that, like advertising, business and other social institutions are riddled with hypocrisy."

The same researchers concluded that such cynicism probably has negative effects on children's attitudes toward business and society, noting, "Children under the age of 13 constitute more than a quarter of the population—that's more than 50 million people who are still learning about our society."[11]

THE GOOD NEWS

Dismayed by TV advertising practices, some citizens organized in order to make change. In 1968 Action for Children's Television (ACT) was created by a group of Massachusetts women to promote quality children's programming *without commercialism*. In 1970 ACT filed a petition with the Federal Communications Commission (FCC) in Washington asking that all commercials be banned from children's programs. After sitting on the issue for years, in 1974, the commission denied the request for rules but instead issued a set of "guidelines" titled *The Policy Statement and Report on Children's Television*.

ACT sued the FCC for refusing to make rules to protect the young and for negotiating with the industry behind closed doors. Acknowledging some abuses, the commission held that the television industry should have another "try" at regulating itself—the spirit of self-regulation being part of the American tradition. Critics still argue that an industry that spends $700 million annually advertising to children can't be counted on to regulate itself.

Feeling the pressure, the industry's National Association of Broadcasters (NAB) revised its code, saying that broadcasters should voluntarily reduce advertising minutes from 16 to 9½ per hour in children's programming, which would bring levels of children's advertising on Saturday and Sunday down to the level of advertising beamed at adults during prime time. Monday-through-Friday children's advertising was reduced to 12 minutes per hour, more than there is on adult prime time. But not all stations complied with the suggestion of self-regulation, and the FCC scheduled a second inquiry (1978–79) into advertising and programming practices for children, presumably with a more serious consideration of regulation.

A most dramatic regulatory action occurred in 1976 when the Federal Trade Commission ordered Spiderman vitamin ads off the air: the consent order that delineated for the first time the commission's views on what constitutes deceptive advertising for products to children on television. The action was significant because it represented the first formal recognition that there is a difference between advertising directed at adults and advertising directed at children.

The FTC's consent order (in response to ACT's complaint) prohibited the Hudson Pharmaceutical Corp. from "directing its advertising for Spiderman and other children's vitamins to child audiences" between 6 A.M. and 9:05 P.M. ACT had argued that the ads, which featured the popular animated Spiderman, "unfairly take advantage of a child's inability to clearly distinguish between fantasy and reality." The FTC staff, in its own complaint, said that "Hudson's practice of directing Spiderman vitamin advertising to children is an unfair and deceptive practice because children are unqualified by age and experience to decide whether or not they need vitamins in general or should use an advertised brand in particular." The consent order stressed that "the use of a hero figure from a popular children's program has the tendency to blur for children the distinction between program content and advertising, and to take advantage of the trust relationship

developed between children and the program character."
According to the FTC, "the use of such a hero figure to endorse
children's vitamins can lead significant numbers of children to
believe that the endorsed product has qualities and characteristics that it does not have." The commission concluded
that "such advertising can induce children to take excessive
amounts of vitamins which can be dangerous to their health."
The pivotal phrase in the report is: "Children are unqualified
by age and experience to decide for themselves whether or not
they need. . . or should use" these vitamins. Written into that
language is the view that children are also unqualified to make
decisions about any other product being advertised.

Other countries can offer the United States an example in
the way that they protect their children from advertising.
Denmark, Norway, Israel, and others permit no ads at all to be
directed at the child audience. Many have strict time and
content limits on advertising—for example, Austria, Italy, and
West Germany—as does the province of Quebec. Strict rules
are enforced by the Quebec Consumer Protection Bureau,
which is made up of representatives of consumer groups,
advertising agencies, and the provincial government. TV ads
in Quebec may not use words that exaggerate the quality,
performance, or durability of a product. The use of superla-
tives to describe a product, of or diminutives to describe
prices—"the best toy," "the greatest game," "the lowest
price"—is forbidden. Nor may the advertising prompt comparisons: "There's nothing else like it," "Nobody else makes
it." In Quebec, ads may not directly urge a child to buy, or to
request another person to buy, a certain product, nor may ads
show "reprehensible" family customs or belittle parental
authority or judgment.

Whether by reason of the products or the practices by which
they are advertised, the case for protecting children from this
selling phenomenon is becoming quite clear. The child advocates' position and its inherent values are summed up elo-
quently by Dr. Richard Feinbloom, in his testimony at the FTC
hearings in early 1979:

> To the industry . . . I have one and only one message: Get out of the business of advertising any of your products to young children. . . . My fundamental objection to treating children as an advertising market does not depend on the content of the advertising. Nor is it basic to my argument that many of the current ads promote expensive, materialistic frivolities and the consumption-oriented mentality in a world in which millions of children go to sleep hungry. . . . It is simply that any decent society should declare young children "off limits" to commercial cultivation.

At some point children have a need to learn the ways of the marketplace and wise consumer behavior. But early childhood is not the arena for learning how to deal with Madison Avenue. To serve the public interest should mean, in part, to protect the rights of children. Children have a basic need for protection from harsh influences of TV advertising—designed by adults for the express purpose of gaining large profits, even at the expense of the young.

▪ 7 ▪
THE
EFFECTS
ON
SOCIAL
RELATIONSHIPS

Children learn what they live.

Dorothy Law Nolte

There's a popular verse on the walls of many homes and pediatricians' offices:

> If a child lives with criticism, he learns to condemn.
> If a child lives with hostility, he learns to fight.
> If a child lives with ridicule, he learns to be shy.
> If a child lives with tolerance, he learns to be patient.
> If a child lives with encouragement, he learns confidence.
> If a child lives with security, he learns to have faith.
> If a child lives with approval, he learns to like himself.
> If a child lives with acceptance and friendship,
>   he learns to find love in the world.

The point is that children learn critical lessons about themselves from their environment without formal instruction. In the past the family, the school, peers, and religion provided the medium for socialization, but increasingly television plays a major part. Sometimes we know TV personalities better than

110

we do our own relatives. As a major agent of socialization, TV teaches children "how the world works and how they should behave in it. What social lessons are our children absorbing when they are in "TV land" for so many hours a day? Individual programs may be good, bad, or indifferent, but what is the *cumulative* experience?

TV presents the child with a distorted definition of reality. The child in the affluent suburb or the small midwestern town exists within his own limited reality. His experience with social problems or people of different races, religions, or nationalities is probably somewhat limited. To the extent that television exposes him to diversity of people and ideas it surely expands the boundaries of his reality. It is precisely because he now relies so heavily on TV to define other realities for him that we must examine so carefully what those images are. If they are distorted, inaccurate, or unfair, then television's reality is potentially harmful.

TV distorts reality by selecting certain kinds of images and omitting others and by portraying people in a stereotyped way. It portrays some categories of people with beauty, power, and importance and renders others weak, helpless, or invisible. So serious is the relative invisibility of some groups on TV that Dr. George Gerbner of the Annenberg School of Communications contends, "If you're not on TV, you don't exist." Yet how often do you see yourself on TV? Or a Hispanic child? The physically handicapped? An intact Black family? The Jewish holidays?

The TV camera selects certain images to be examples, sometimes functioning like a magnifying glass held up to the worst in civilization instead of the best. When TV producers focus on violent ugliness, they lift it out and hold it up for all to see, making it impressively larger than life. A fistfight that occurs outside my window and is witnessed by only five people may be videotaped, broadcast, and "witnessed" vicariously by millions of people, thus multiplying the example set by the fistfighters. In the United States, most people have not witnessed murder, yet because of television most children have seen hundreds of thousands of violent deaths and therefore believe that the world is more violent than it actually is.

"For many people the relatively passive acceptance of TV fare defines what is typical, what is desirable, what is probable, and what is possible," says Dr. Chester Pierce, psychiatrist at Harvard University. "In fact, lower-income people, minorities and children may be more likely to believe that what they see on TV represents reality."[1]

TV says, in effect: This is the way the world works. These are the rules. The images presented on TV tend to be exaggerated or glorified, and so believed and accepted as models to be copied. One demonstration of such TV power to influence behavior became apparent during Evel Knievel's heavily promoted attempt to "fly" his motorcyle over the Snake River. Many children imitated his stunts with their bicycles on homemade ramps. And many landed in hospitals. "The kids are really caught up in the Evel fervor," said one doctor. "The television carried a special on Saturday night just before he made his big jump, showing him jumping over 10 garbage trucks or whatever he does, and this is what the kids are trying to imitate." Even the children who did not see Evel Knievel took up the bike jumping because they, in turn, caught the idea from friends who had been watching the Knievel TV promotion.

TV affects human relationships as well as behavior by influencing our feelings about ourselves and our expectations for ourselves and others. Too frequently stereotypes provide us with instant definitions. The stereotype assigns to an individual characteristics associated with a group that may or may not be accurate. We tend to note a single feature of a person and fill in the details from a storehouse of stereotypes.

Psychologist Joyce Sprafkin says of stereotypes: "Overall TV appears to be a somewhat dramatized, but accurate representation of the non-TV world. However, like the funhouse mirror, television actually reflects characteristics which are unquestionably ours, but with distortions which may not be entirely laughable."[2]

Via TV's stereotypes we see men as strong and active,

women pretty and at home. All too frequently, minorities are cast in exaggerated portrayals and stereotyped roles, more as white male producers perceive them than the way minority persons perceive themselves.

Exposure to stereotyped presentations can easily influence viewers' behavior toward unfamiliar people. Viewers use what they learn from these TV images to establish norms for how they will act in certain situations. These images, in fact, teach values and behaviors, especially to children who have little firsthand knowledge of the real world. To the extent that children are exposed to certain character portrayals and behaviors on TV, they may acquire or learn those behaviors and roles and eventually accept them as models for their own attitudes and actions.

Perhaps most serious are the effects of information distortions on the child's self-image. At some level we begin to judge our own meaning, dignity, and worth in comparison with the TV characters who portray people like us. How accurate or fair is this barrage of portrayals that we are exposed to each day? What are the portrayals teaching about racial minorities, family relationships, sexuality?

According to TV, how does the world in fact work?

SEX ROLES AND RELATIONSHIPS ON TV

Sexuality involves an integrated sense of self as male or female as well as perceptions of what it is for others to be male or female, man or woman. As Elizabeth Roberts of the Harvard Project on Human Sexuality expresses it: "Sexuality is expressed through our lifestyles, our social roles, in the ways we express affection and intimacy, as well as through our erotic behaviors and attitudes toward the social and economic consequences of our sexual conduct. Human sexuality is expressed in the full range of interactions with others."

Whether we are talking about sexuality as a whole, erotic sex, sex roles, or sexism, we can find many stereotypical examples of each in the study of television.

The sexes are portrayed in a lopsided way on TV, both in

numbers and pictures. Women, who make up over 50 percent of the population, comprise less than 30 percent of the characters on prime-time television. White males fill over 60 percent of these roles, while they actually represent about 40 percent of the population. The percentage of minority women presented on TV is less than half their representation in real life.[3]

Children's programming reflects the same biases. In a 1977 analysis of children's Saturday morning and weekday afternoon programming by F. Earle Barcus, noted researcher at Boston University, only one out of every four characters was female. Sixty percent of the characters in the commercials carried on those programs were male. (Non-Black minorities were rarely portrayed in either commercials or programs. About 9 percent of the program segments depicted elderly persons, and only 9 of 899 characters were handicapped.)[4]

The relative invisibility of certain groups is probably in itself assimilated by children; but, in case it isn't, the nature of the portrayals they do see can reinforce the message. What are people *doing* on the screen?

Typically, women are shown as fluffy, addicted consumers who do not figure in the action of the program other than as counterpoint to the male hero. Women on TV are twice as likely to exhibit incompetent behavior as men. The spokespersons in commercials—the authoritative voices that speak for the product—are overwhelmingly male and almost always white. A study of network news programs by the U.S. Civil Rights Commission found no minority newsmakers used as "experts" on any topic. Female experts spoke only on women's issues.[5]

Women are defined in status by their relationship to men. And although women make up about 40 percent of the nation's labor force, only a minor percentage of TV's females have a definite occupational activity other than as "slave" to man. One of the most outrageous examples is Jeannie (on *I Dream of Jeannie*), a curvy blonde in the service of a "master" who can summon her appearance or existence by snapping his fingers. Upon arrival she will first inquire, "Master, what can I do for you?" Her function is to wait on him, get him out of embarrassing situations, amuse him, or otherwise satisfy his needs. She is a glamorous slave, and her portrayal is made so appealing that the program, it seems, is one of the most popular among boys and girls of four to ten years of age.

Another extremely popular program that makes typical stereotypical statements about men and women is *The Flintstones*, an animated cartoon series that employs a prehistoric setting for stories about domestic life (which are intended to bear striking resemblance to those of modern suburbia). The "hero," Fred, is portrayed as a bumbling idiot, and Mrs. Flintstone is portrayed as a manipulative bitch. A major element in the communication on *The Flintstones* is Fred's all-purpose idiot cry, "Yabba dabba doo."

Due to immaturity or lack of experience, children are especially vulnerable to the social lessons of such stereotypes. Research by Charles Atkin and Bradley Greenberg at Michigan State University illustrated that children's perceptions of males and females generally corresponded to the stereotypes found on TV. Men were seen as strong, knowledgeable, able to give orders and solve problems. Women were seen primarily as having problems and getting upset. But when children watched programs in which women played a strong role in society, their image of real-world women was more positive.[6]

To see men cast as activists and women as the spectators shapes young boys' and girls' sexuality and attitudes about sexuality. Elizabeth Roberts puts it this way:

> When television viewers see men giving respect to each other for being violent, controlling or unemotional, when they see women relate to each other only through men, when they see unmarried women primarily as victims, married men primarily as fools, and children with "asexual" parents, they are receiving clear sexual messages about "appropriate" sexual conduct. Television's focus on the relationships between people may be far more important and have far more impact on the sexual scripts of children and adults than the portrayal of any particular nude scene or sexual act.

Yet television tells us that:

- Sex can sell everything from toothpaste ("It gives your mouth sex appeal") to automobiles. Beautiful young women in revealing outfits adorn every type of commercial from stereo ads to hotel ads.
- Sex is not for married people. An analysis of one week of programs found that the sex act most frequently implied was heterosexual intercourse between unmarried people. Intercourse between married partners was indicated far less often. Prostitution was suggested more frequently than sex between married people! Whether or not this is the view most parents would like their children to have, this is the view children, and especially adolescents, are getting from TV.
- Sex is a weapon to wield power over others. In crime shows, drama, and situation comedies, sex is often an instrument of control. Famed female cops and detectives use their physical charms as effectively as their revolvers in order to lure the criminal. Similarly, sex is used as a weapon to "close a deal" or "make a sale."

While TV's role as sex educator has increased, parental involvement in actively teaching about sexuality is virtually absent. Children receive a major part of their education about sexuality from watching TV. A study by The Project on Human Sexual Development showed that in spite of so-called liberation, parents today don't feel any more free to discuss sex with their children than parents of the former generation. In a study of 1,400 Cleveland parents with children age three to fourteen, researchers found that most parents would talk to their children in simple terms about pregnancy and physical differences between the sexes but that few spoke of intercourse, contraception, venereal disease, intimacy, or sexual values. Around 90 percent of the parents said they had never discussed any aspect of erotic behavior or its consequences. Many who discussed procreation spoke in terms of "the birds and the bees" or some other metaphor.

Despite soaring rates of teen-age pregnancy, children get

little solid information and explanation about sexuality from responsible sources. But they do learn a great deal through TV, typically by suggestion and stereotypes rather than by carefully explained information. The parents in the Cleveland study realized this. They said that television and the movies were a main provider of whatever sexual awareness their children had. This suggests that the young are receiving a dangerously incomplete and distorted education about sexuality upon which they will base their own social and sexual relationships.

Occasionally, television has made commendable attempts at sex education in programs such as ABC's *The Birth of a Baby* and *My Mom's Having a Baby.* Joint viewing of these programs by parent and child could extend the potential positive effects of TV. While a careful search might turn up positive, useful, and instructive images about sexuality—ideas which could help build wholesome self-identity—the fare that turns up with the spin of the dial cannot be labeled healthy for the growth of sexuality in young people.

RACIAL MINORITIES

A Black writer remembers:

> In the mid-1960s, long before the creation of "family viewing time," a television phenomenon existed that brought my entire family happily together in front of our small screen. The big event was the appearance of a black person on a television program. Whether as a walk-on character in a commercial, a bit-part in a drama, or a two-minute act in a variety-entertainment show, "one of us" on the tube was a rare enough occasion to warrant the cessation of all household operations. Mother, Father, Auntie and kids would snuggle together, side-by-side in front of the TV, each intently absorbing this major affirmation that blacks were indeed real people who used American products, and existed in other parts of the world. Unlike the network family viewing hours, which are regularly scheduled each evening, our family viewing

was impromptu and infrequent. In 1962, for example, only three black faces appeared once every five hours in one television sample.[7]

Blacks were not the only people who were "invisible" to TV viewers. Native Americans, Asian Americans, Hispanic Americans appeared even less often than Blacks on TV. All together, minority groups constituted less than 3 percent of all characters in televised dramas and comedies as recently as the mid-1970's.

In the late 1970's a study of children's TV programming by F. Earle Barcus showed that nine out of ten characters were white. Blacks on children's TV were most often represented on comedy and variety programs and were more likely to be portrayed as children than as teen-agers or adults. In one study of prime time, both Blacks and women were given a disproportionately high number of immature, demeaning, and comical roles, with Blacks often depicted as lovable buffoons, servants, or dancers.[8]

Racism (and sexism) are conveyed in a variety of subtle ways, both verbal and nonverbal—the quality of a person's speech, the villain's foreign accent, who interrupts whom, who keeps his or her "cool" in tense situations, who solves the problems. In various content analyses, whites and males come out ahead.

Chester Pierce, a Black psychiatrist, points out that the way prejudiced behaviors are spread by television is by "subtle, stunning, often automatic and non-verbal exchanges which are put-downs of Blacks by offenders. The cumulative weight of their never-ending burden is the major ingredient in Black —white interactions."

In one study, Pierce and colleagues analyzed TV commercials, coding behaviors and portrayals, noting that one would predict from this sample that Blacks would

1. be seen less frequently than animals.
2. never teach whites.
3. be seen to eat more frequently than whites.

4. have fewer positive contacts with each other.
5. have less involvement in family life.
6. more often work for wages.
7. not live in the suburbs.
8. entertain others.
9. never initiate or control actions, situations, or events.
10. have less command of technology.
11. have less command of space.

Pierce concludes:

> It is our view that TV is but one of a plethora of sources which spew out microaggressions through offensive mechanisms to Blacks. In media alone, such micro-aggressions are daily occurrences in newspapers, radio programs, films, billboards, subway posters, textbooks, statues, and so on. Once a child, black or white, can diagnose these microaggressions and diagnose offensive maneuvers, the child will think differently and perhaps behave differently. . . . TV exerts immense influence in training people how to act toward other races and how other races should act toward them. When everyone is made aware of this training process, it may mean that ways can be found to alter it so as to insure more harmonious and just human relations."[9]

Yet blatant stereotypes will continue to plague us in the context of reruns and old movies. Made before the national and network consciousnesses were raised, they remain an important source of programming for independent stations. They often fill daytime hours when children are watching. Sadly, it can still be said that our children's primary sources of knowledge of Native Americans are typified by F-Troop and old cowboy movies.

Charles Atkin and Bradley Greenberg's research (cited earlier) showed that white children, especially those in suburban or rural areas with few contacts with Black people, reported that most of what they knew about Blacks came from what they saw on television. Incredibly, Greenberg's sample of

Black children said that they obtained most of their knowledge about how Black people dress, behave, and talk from TV rather than from their real-life experiences. And Blacks were more likely than whites to believe that Black characters were realistically portrayed.

IMAGES OF FAMILIES

If kids take their ideas about what is true, probable, and possible from TV, what are they learning about families today? In the early days of TV, *Mama* (CBS, 1949–56) gave America its first TV portrait of family. Peggy Wood played the immigrant matriarch from Norway who, with her husband, learned to adapt to American ways through their three children. The show dealt with the problems of turn-of-the-century youth that could be resolved by parental wisdom and family love.

TV's contemporary family portrait includes little love and shows scarcely an intact family. Rather, family life on TV is notably absent. Rose Goldsen, sociology professor at Cornell University, found few heart-warming images in her study of six months of prime-time family shows (1974–75). Two-thirds of the programs featured characters who had no noticeable family relations at all, or, if a family tie was mentioned, it was an off-stage one. Many of these prime-time programs were crime-and-action adventure shows; only two featured twentieth-century families in which a mother and father were raising their own children *(Apple's Way* and *Good Times).* Single parents and families consisting of adults exclusively were common. Goldsen concludes, "Images of any emotionally meaningful life in an intact family are almost nonexistent. The few programs that feature people who live in complete families . . . are typically historical dramas or 'sitcoms.' The historical dramas show an intact family as if it were a relic of this country's past."[10]

Popular prime-time shows that feature families include *The Waltons* on CBS, which concerns the struggles of a large, close-knit family in Appalachia during the Depression; *The Brady Bunch,* a syrup-sweet comedy series about a young widow and widower who marry and merge their families—six cheerful children and a housekeeper; *The Jeffersons*, centering on a middle-class Black family in a luxury apartment building; and *All in the Family*, a landmark series that opened situation comedies to "mature themes and frank dialogue" built on the clashes of bigot Archie Bunker and his liberal son-in-law. Typically, Bunker and his son-in-law, Mike (like J.J. and his sister on *Good Times*), trade verbal barbs for 30 minutes a week without leaving any noticeable scars.

In or out of family context, put-down humor is an element that we have allowed television to impose on our lives. Dignity and respect are abandoned in a game of one-upmanship. (One of TV's memorable contributions to our children's vocabulary in recent years was "Up your nose with a rubber hose.")

In daytime television, soap operas are "anti-family dramas," says Dr. Rose Goldsen. Her six-month count of images in the soaps yielded 15 marriages, 19 shackings-up, and 19 separations or divorces (either final, threatening, or under consideration). Numerous pairings smacked of incest—and the triangle made up of mother, daughter, and the same man was not unusual, notes Goldsen.

What the soaps have to say about children does not lift the spirit either. Goldsen writes:

> . . . the serials picture conception, pregnancy, gestation and birth as such chancy matters . . . as troublesome, scary, fraught with danger, laden with unimaginable dread. Suppose a daytime serial woman finds out she's pregnant. The chances are about 7 to 10 that she's not married to the father or that the pregnancy is unwelcome to one or both of the parents—the result of accident, thoughtlessness, deception, or rape. It's 7 to 10 again that the fetus won't make it through to term.

In the study, Goldsen found 11 pregnancies which resulted in two miscarriages, two abortions under consideration, and three births which were almost fatal to the mother. Only one pregnancy in the six months of TV involved a woman and man who were married to each other and living together in reasonable harmony. It is likely that soaps injure the image of family commitment by a visual code that implicitly denies that children are important in family living.

EFFECTS ON FAMILY RELATIONSHIPS

Although family life as portrayed on TV is far from realistic, many children use TV family portrayals as a source of information about family relationships. If children's expectations are gleaned from The Brady Bunch (where the beds are always made, meals are on time, the housekeeper is handy, and parents are blissfully happy), they may feel that their own families are inadequate. If their notions of marriage are taken from the soaps (where relationships cause only problems), they may vow not to engage in such relationships.

Even more serious effects may result from what TV viewing itself does to family living patterns. While earlier generations had the notion that the TV set was drawing families together, about 50 percent of U.S. households today have more than one set, a phenomenon that tends to create a pattern of isolation. Mom and Dad can watch what they want in the living room while the kids watch what they please in the bedroom or TV room. There is no impetus to discuss what to watch, no need to sit in the same room, less chance to supervise what the kids see, no opportunity to interpret content for them or observe their reactions. Even the illusion of togetherness is lost.

It was once thought that the effect of TV viewing would be modified by the "pattern of influences" that already existed in the home. But today those influences are themselves molded by television. Families do not tend to set up rituals, activities, and communication patterns and then see how television fits into them. Television is there from the beginning, determining the form these patterns will take. TV is not simply one of many influences, it is the organizing influence.

The quality of family life depends largely on what a family does. Many important family rituals and activities are usurped by the presence of television and the pull of the TV viewing habit. When we consider that family members often spend more time "relating" to the tube than to each other, perhaps we should consider TV not so much an intruder as an adopted member of the family—a member who is given a central position in the household, is present at many meals, has become organizer of family holiday rituals, is the focus of bedtime routines, and spends about six hours a day communicating to various other members of the family.

Just as the arrival of a new baby alters the relationships between family members, so does the presence of a TV affect the lives of those in the television household. Watching television is the primary leisure-time activity in the United States. It consumes so many hours per day that little time is left to pursue other activities. Walks, talks, guessing games, sleep-time rituals, and many spontaneous activities are reduced. Families who would have read aloud to each other or played Monopoly to fill the hours between dinner and bedtime now achieve the illusion of togetherness by sitting down in the same room (sometimes) and watching TV together.

Dinnertime, once a chance to "catch up" on everyone's daily activities and cares, tends to be given over to the news or reruns of *The Odd Couple*. Bedtime is not 8:30 but "right after *Happy Days*," or later. Neilsen ratings show that 20 percent of children six to eleven years old are still watching at 10:30. Homework may be done before the set and teeth are brushed during commercials. Bedtime stories are not delivered with a hug and a smile from mother or father but come with a laugh track and a Lysol ad from the box in the corner.

Television not only replaces activities, it replaces communication within the family. Families may be physically together while watching certain programs, but they do not necessarily talk to each other. They do not even look at each other. If a caring adult should ask a question in the middle of a program, typically one child says nothing and the other says "S-h-h-h." TV holds the eyes and fills in the silences, and by filling the silences it often creates a void in family relationships. The more television takes over family time and conversation, the less time there is to pursue other activities from which to draw subsequent family conversation—and the more TV itself becomes the topic.

Increasingly, play and "caper" are "programmed out" by many hours a day of TV viewing. Meals are set up against a backdrop of TV messages (along with TV tables, TV dinners, TV rooms). Celebrations, parties, and holidays are often upstaged by a "media event" such as a TV "special" or a football game.

People who decide to live without TV for a while notice the impact on family life. Participants in one study said: "It became easier to bathe the kids. When we had the TV on, nobody wanted to take a bath—we were all afraid we'd miss something." Another said, "Our sex life increased about 50 percent for the simple reason that we went to bed earlier and together." One father said he was "nervous and bored and smoking twice as much." Many said that they turned instead to movies, board games, eating out, sewing, going to the circus, etc.[11]

TV CREATES FAMILY CONFLICT

In addition to its negative effect on family living patterns, TV viewing may actually create active conflicts in the family. Differences arise over how much to watch, what to watch, and when to watch (at 7 A.M.? 10 P.M.? When grandmother is coming? During meals? When there's homework?) Expensively produced, persuasive commercials cause unnecessary stress in families and put parents in the position of frequently saying "no" to the children's repeated demands. Many a battle is fought in the cereal aisles of America's supermarkets as children who are small enough to ride in the shopping carts proclaim their preference for Fruity Pebbles or Cookie Crisp over mother's choice of oatmeal. As one consumer advocate testified before the Federal Trade Commission, "Where is it written that the new family structure should be parent, child and General Foods?" While parents may, of course, say "no" to kids' TV-induced demands, having to say "no" so often puts unreasonable strain on the parent–child relationship.

On a broader level, TV can create stress in a family when the values and messages emanating from the set do not coincide with those the parents are trying to teach. If a family advocates materialism, rigid sex roles, racial stereotypes, casual sex, and violence, it will have few qualms about TV functioning as a moral educator. Fortunately, these are not the values of millions of families. When two major agents of socialization send out such conflicting messages, it can create anxiety in the child and make the parents' job difficult.

This problem is aggravated by the growth of multiset households. Research has shown that parental intervention and interpretation of television content, even simple expressions of approval or disapproval, can influence the effect of that content on children. Unfortunately, most children watch alone, and the presence of two or more sets in a household promotes this.

RELATIONSHIPS TO PEERS

Young children who spend a great deal of time passively watching television are not relating to each other. "Relating," like other skills, requires both *interaction* and *practice*. Because habitual TV viewing affects the nature of play, expectations about others, and attitudes about oneself, it also affects how kids make friends. As discussed earlier, *play* helps children learn many vital affective and cognitive skills. TV frequently acts as a substitute for play. Four-to-eight-year-olds in particular, who otherwise might go outside and play after school, often get caught up in the spell of the afternoon cartoons and never make it out the door. Even when friends come over they may forego play for *The Flintstones*, although watching TV would seem to defeat the purpose of a social visit.

Several studies have shown that young persons classified as insecure in their peer-group relationships—children who had difficulty making friends or interacting within a group—were found to be heavy television viewers. Whether TV is a cause or a balm for this insecurity is uncertain, but it is clear that TV touches the relationships between children in many ways, and no child is immune. Even parents who regulate what their children watch soon discover that the kids know all about last night's *Starsky and Hutch*—from their friends. Many a parent has been heard to say he or she would love to dispense with the set altogether but "doesn't want the kids to feel left out."

In addition to limiting social contacts, television viewing may even affect the general *outlook* that colors children's social relationships. As discussed in Chapter 6, by age twelve, TV children tend to develop considerable cynicism about television commercials. They discover that they've been "used" by advertising, and they're not very willing to let that happen routinely. There is concern that this cynicism carries over to other institutions as well, as kids generalize that people, like ads, deceive them.

Televised violence leaves its mark on the child's outlook, as well. When school children were asked how often it is "all right" to hit someone you're mad at, heavy viewers were far more likely than light viewers to respond that it was "almost always all right." Heavy viewers were also more likely to say that they would be afraid to walk alone in a city at night.[12] In another study, children who were heavy viewers were found to be twice as likely as light viewers to feel "scared often."[13] Television leaves a residue of fear and mistrust which does not provide an ideal basis for forming healthy, productive personal relationships.

Mr. Rogers is one children's television performer who emphasizes positive values and stresses principles of human dignity and neighborliness. But these examples of the positive use of TV are the exception, not the rule. Most children's TV is loaded with sexual and racial stereotypes, violence, and fear messages, as children see an enormous amount of programming that is geared for adults. Stereotypes may be assimilated via families, peers, and children's books, but TV rates high as an influence.

RELATIONSHIP TO SELF

How you feel about yourself influences how you will respond and relate to others. TV affects human relationships by influencing our feelings about ourselves and our expectations for ourselves and others. Expectations, in turn, influence behavior.

As children watch television, they internalize what they see. They are willing to let the TV image answer the question Who am I?, and they are willing to let TV people be models for their own behavior. Moreover, television affects children's ideas of their own abilities and potential. Psychologist Dr. Sherryl Graves says:

> Children develop a sense of themselves not only from their interactions with family members, teachers and friends, but their sense of self is influenced by the reflections of people like themselves that society presents. Clearly television's characterizations of female, black and minority or foreign born people don't suggest positive evaluations by the society-at-large.[14]

Television tells girls, minority, and foreign children that people like themselves are minimally important segments of the society because they are not recognized (pictured) on TV. The fact that Hispanic, Asian, and Native American group members are presented so infrequently may suggest to them that they are insignificant in the overall picture of life. The portrayal of these groups represents the degree of respect that the groups are given by society. Since most of the money, prestige, and status are assigned to white males, all others conclude that their group rightfully occupies an inferior status.

While there has been little solid research on the impact of television on the self-concept of viewers, it is Dr. Graves' interpretation of existing surveys that heavy viewers are more likely to report greater dissatisfaction with self than do light viewers.

Television *can* expose children to people and aspects of life that they may not be able to experience directly. Programs designed to present positive portrayals of minority groups, such as *Sesame Street, Vegetable Soup, Fat Albert,* and *Big Blue Marble,* can be highly effective in increasing positive racial attitudes and information in the young. Dr. Graves reports that viewers of *Big Blue Marble,* compared with nonviewers, were more likely to perceive foreign children as healthy, happy and "better off," and less likely to express feelings of superiority of American children.

As the verse at the beginning of this chapter suggests, the child who lives with approval and encouragement learns to like himself and have confidence. Part of the adult's analysis of the TV that children see should ask: Does this viewing experience help the child toward self-esteem? What is there in this program that will help the child feel good and confident?

WORLD VIEW

These concerns about TV would not be worth fussing about if TV's influence did not affect human relationships.

TV erodes our private image. How we see the world is affected by our sense of our own position in society, and television changes that position by letting us see from different points in time and space.

When new technologies let us view our planet from outer space, it lured us away from the idea that the earth and its people are the center of the universe. Similarly, *Roots* let us stand in the shoes of a slave and have a look from inside that culture. And when television brought the napalm-flaming villages of Vietnam into every American household, the "living-room war" became a hotter political issue at home. Some say that because television brought American citizens a new perspective on Vietnam, the mood of the people was affected, and ultimately the citizenry insisted on the cessation of fighting.

To the extent that TV creates fair and accurate portrayals, it expands collective understanding. One diplomat feels that TV is helpful to people in provincial areas because it exposes them to global affairs. Before television we would never hear people on the streets of, say, Fort Dodge, Iowa, talking about Afghanistan or Upper Volta. But that has changed. Marshall McLuhan said that TV images from around the world would create a "global village" in which everybody could respond quickly to each other's daily lives.

While there may be more images from afar, however, the type of image may do little to increase our wisdom. Earthquakes and executions will win out over a story about, say, health care innovations in Mexico, thereby reinforcing negative images of the world beyond our borders.

As we develop awareness of effects, we can develop a new consciousness about "justice" and "fairness" in TV portrayals. Some stations have ceased to air certain old movies—frequently film classics from the 1930's—because they are offensive to minority groups and others whose awareness cannot embrace what they see to be promiscuous use of ethnic stereotypes for gags or gratuitous violence for entertainment. Under attack, for example, are the war films of the 1940's in which Japanese and Germans were ridiculed or represented as evil or vicious.

As Les Brown explained in a *New York Times* story, sensitivities vary from city to city, depending on their ethnic components. A film such as John Huston's *The Treasure of Sierra Madre* may be kept off the air in areas with large communities of Mexican-Americans but will play elsewhere in the country without significant protest. That film seems most offensive in the Southwest because the villain is a despicable but comic Mexican bandit. His role was so organic to the film that it could not be edited without destroying the story.

Similarly, Chinese-American communities resent the Charlie Chan pictures, while others are offended by certain Western movies that portray the American Indian as unfairly aggressive.

As we gain understanding about the power of picture media and the socialization process, we should be asking ourselves which images we want to feed to young children. Moreover, we might ask what kinds of children we want to raise to meet the needs of the future. Do we want them to be patient, confident, self-assured, and loving? What else might we hope for?

But even as we are wishing for resensitization and respect for life, most of us watch more and more television each year—where our feelings are being dulled. In spite of tenaciously held hopes for the future of powerful communications technology in America—the world's richest nation—today's television is the purveyor of demeaning criticism, hostility, ridicule, sexual abuse, and intolerance. This is the way it is happening. And all our children are watching!

▪ 8 ▪
ACTION
AT
HOME

*Today's children are raised
not only by their parents,
but by complex educational
and medical systems,
by the flickering electronic
babysitter of television
and by the marketing and regulatory
policies that permit the use of
poorly tested food additives. . . .
Similar social forces lie behind
most major shifts in today's families.
Parents are not abdicating—
they are being dethroned
by pressures over which they have
little direct influence or control.*

Kenneth Keniston
Carnegie Council on Children

Like their elders, most of today's parents care deeply about their children's growth. They want to share in it—and shape it. They know that early experiences make a great difference in what will happen later. While parenting is often fun, it is harder to be a parent today than ever in the past. We have to deal not only with the age-old dilemmas of toilet training and sibling rivalry—but with aspects of massive and rapid change: the loss of a known world, the sexual revolution, the drug culture, and the ever-present flickering of zillions of television sets.

Parents sense that TV is especially stripping them of their control and affecting the way in which they raise their children. They sense that habitual TV viewing affects the way kids think and behave. They want to know: Will TV viewing make my children aggressive? Can it teach them to read? To think? To imagine? To make judgments? Can TV teach kids to care? Millions of parents have wondered about these questions—and so have I. As a writer and teacher, I have absorbed the research, but there is little in the research that tells a parent directly what to do. Since our elders cannot tell us or show us how to raise children with TV or how to deal with rapid change, who then can be our guide?

We have insufficient guidance. And we really cannot give "answers" to other people's viewing dilemmas. *But we can learn from each other.* We can experiment to find out which uses of TV benefit children's growth. We can invent ways to use TV wisely at home. We can share what we learn, including our mistakes. We must take cues from each other's experience.

One way to begin is to ask again: What are the basic needs of children? How might television serve those needs?

Children have a basic need

to trust.
to relate to people.
to use the senses and whole body.
to pay attention.
to release their innate imagery.
to play.
to develop physical skills.
to be free of fear.
to master appropriate technology, *i.e.*, tools which they can learn to use.
to be protected from inappropriate technology, *i.e.*, tools which they can't learn how to use when they are young.

GETTING STARTED

Most parents have little idea how much TV is watched at home. The average day of a typical four-year-old boy goes something like this: He eats breakfast with *Captain Kangaroo* and then watches *Sesame Street* and might catch part of the game shows in the morning. In the afternoon he watches some reruns of *Batman, Star Trek,* or *The Brady Bunch* or sometimes (at his mother's urging) watches *Sesame* again. During supper the family often watches the local news (last night: spotlight on teen-age vandalism), and later he'll watch whatever is on. Weekends, while his parents sleep, he is quietly tucked in front of the TV, filling up on cookies and cartoons. A few hours a day quickly add up to over 30 hours a week, exactly what the A. C. Nielsen Company says is routine for most American kids.

One way to take stock of TV viewing is to keep a journal, or a list, of all the TV consumed by a person in a given week. Like counting calories, there are hidden bits and pieces that add up. Once the amount of intake is measured, it can be analyzed and possibly changed.

And while the pencil is handy, it is important to add up the real-life experiences, too. Do they balance up with the vicarious "experiences"? Do you read aloud to your children? How many hours a week? Do you talk to your child? What do you talk about? Do you take the toddler outside to explore or play and encourage (or insist) that older children play outdoors for a part of each day? Do you take walks or field trips? What are your family rituals? Do you celebrate holidays and birthdays? Are naptime and bedtime ceremonies part of the child's day? How are ideas expressed? What kinds of sensory activities are part of life at home? Do you cook together, make things, build, fix, sing, sew, dance, swim, jog, play games, plant vegetables? Do you eat meals together? What does the family talk about? Laugh about? Do family members each have some "quiet time" alone—to rest, daydream, imagine?

Do you use TV to keep your children occupied while you have work to do? Do you wait on them, bringing snacks? Do children eat meals before the set? When the kids are home sick, do they watch TV all day?

A broad base of real-life experience is a person's best resource in viewing TV critically; the child with many kinds of experiences will bring to the screen a natural interpreting ability as soon as maturity permits. The most effective way to achieve critical viewing skills in people of all ages is to insure that they have an abundance of experience, particularly sensory experience. To take the first steps toward using TV wisely, parents can

broaden real-life experience.
limit TV viewing time.
evaluate TV content.
introduce TV as an instructional tool.
talk about the TV children watch.
listen to children's responses to TV.
join a parent-support group.
communicate their TV policies to the local school.

BROADENING REAL-LIFE EXPERIENCE

Parents who expand direct experience by limiting vicarious experience and by focusing on a few basic guidelines usually find that TV becomes a friend, not a foe.

Establish structure. In order to feel secure, children need some predictable *structuring* of both time and space. To structure time, a parent can develop sets of regularly repeated real-life activities—scheduled meals together, naptimes for young ones, bedtimes, story times, walks, talks. Such rituals structure time and tend to tie the participants together. Adults can help children grow by *using* time creatively rather than merely letting TV *fill up* time.

Space at home can also be structured and can thereby affect life-styles. For example, the placement of TV sets can dictate the family's use of space and time. If there are three sets in three separate rooms there will be more TV viewing in the household and that viewing will tend to occur not in groups but in isolation.

Built into the time/space structure should be some free time and privacy for each person—that is, free from TV and free from other scheduled activity. Reflecting on this idea, one mother said, "Yesterday I noticed Peter on the floor just lying on his back holding a paper airplane over his head. He stayed that way for about 20 minutes. I could have been tempted to urge him to *do something*, but I stopped myself because I know that it's healthy for children to daydream and have some leisure."

Encourage physical exercise of all kinds. Running; jumping; climbing; building things; feeling the water, the sand, the substance are physical activities that will encourage the use of the eyes, hands, and whole body in ways that promote learning abilities and ease tensions or hyperactivity. Too often parents separate the mental and physical aspects of learning. Kids who develop skills through exercise will participate more in games and sports as they get older and will not stand off because of a lack of confidence or comfort themselves with hours of undemanding TV viewing.

Encourage play. Play may be the best learning activity of all, no matter what its form. If their time and attention is not usurped by TV, children find forms of play and cook up countless games. Kickball, stick ball, chase games, and other made-up games such as "Going to Florida" and "Garbage Can Tennis" are played up, down, and around the block wherever they are encouraged.

Sometimes parents of preschoolers start a play group to encourage play and meet some social needs. A friend and I once started a basement play group which included eight children. It was successful partly because it relied on simple hands-on material which stimulated the children to their own creativity—no precut Halloween pumpkins and valentines. We used "junk scrap"—cereal boxes, egg cartons, milk containers, wood scrap—as well as wet clay, powdered paint, washtubs filled with water, boats, blocks, paper, crayons, and flour-and-water paste (that the children measured and made). We collected items to make a housekeeping corner and a book corner.

We encouraged body movement with song and rhyme and did number plays, finger plays, marching, jumping, clapping, and dance. The children learned to sit at a table at juice time, pouring and measuring their own juice ("half-cup" became a part of their working vocabulary). We planted vegetables and watched them grow (it takes time!), and we played outdoors every day. An excellent guide for parents to this type of activity is *The Play Group Book* by Marie Winn.

Select toys which foster creativity. These are toys of "low definition," which don't tell the child exactly how they should be employed in play: teddy bears, balls, blocks, boxes, blanket tents, cloth tunnels, scraps of all kinds, Lego, dolls, jump ropes, sand, clay, paint. TV toys (Batman, Barbie Dolls, *Star Wars* apparatus) tend to suggest a specific kind of play; the child merely copies whatever the toy "does" on TV. Also, when making a purchase be sure to look closely at the toy and handle it. In times past, people could do this easily. But today's toys are showcased and demonstrated on the TV screen (often deceptively), then come into stores and discount houses in sealed containers. To know what you are buying, ask to examine the toy.

Be a model and teacher for the child's imaginative behavior. Sometimes it seems that creativity runs in families—or classrooms. To some extent it does. Creativity is contagious and can be "caught" by being near a person who behaves creatively or who prompts you to be inventive or playful. Nothing is a better catalyst to children's creativity than an adult who genuinely enjoys what the child is doing.

Adults can learn behaviors that promote imagination in the children around them, say psychologists Dorothy and Jerome Singer in *Partners in Play.* They recommend revving up your own imagination by keeping a log of your dreams or by writing a paragraph a day about your feelings. Try to do something new each week—as an experiment, bake bread, make birthday cards, learn something "all new." If you truly enjoy your own creative efforts, that will speak to children more clearly than any lesson. Play is an attitude.

They suggest participating in children's games, but carefully. First, watch kids play to see what their play themes are and how they deal with preoccupations. Sometimes children lure you into their play. Say the Singers:

> The art is to maintain your adult status while going along with the game. To play at make-believe you may have to unbend a little, imitate different voices or sound effects, or get down on the floor to avoid overwhelming the child by either your size or your better motor coordination. At the same time you have to avoid acting too "childish." A child is confused and distressed if he witnesses adults losing their dignity or behaving like a "baby." You can enter into the game with gusto, but try to play a somewhat more adult role—captain of a ship, a large animal, a friendly giant.

Finally, the Singers recommend stimulating children by initiating a play idea. This might happen by telling a story or by gathering a set of toys, tools, utensils, or other materials. Enthusiasm is contagious—"This is going to be a great game."

Encourage social relationships. Learning to interact, to share, to compromise, to respond, to participate are important; this begins in communication with parents. Not only do social relationships make for general happiness, but one major study shows that the boys who had good communication with their parents were least apt to imitate TV violence. Communication may be thought of as a form of protection.

Communication can occur while preparing breakfast or doing errands, or in more specific situations centered around a child's special activity. We have an institution at our house called bed talk; this is when I sit on the edge of the child's bed and listen to whatever the child wants to talk about. Even as they grow up and turn into rough-and-tumble soccer players, I see that they ask for "bed talk"—the comfort of a personal conversation.

Children should be taught how to relate to other children and adults, too. The more *time* children spend with people, not machines, the easier it will be to develop these skills. Do your children watch TV at mealtimes, at parties, at school, when they might be relating to other persons?

Provide good nutrition at home. The parents's job as "nutrition educator" gets harder and harder as TV viewing increases, because children see so many junk food ads. Early experience with healthy high-protein foods will increase the child's familiarity and appetite for them and decrease the space in the stomach for empty calories and nonnutritious "foods." It is much easier to provide a good diet if you do not take young children to the supermarket with you where they inevitably nag for products you don't want to buy. It may be worth the price of a babysitter. Many times it is necessary to take children along, and in this case the adult shopper must remember how to say no firmly (but with love). It may help to take one last look at your shopping cart just before you check out to count up the snacking items and sugar foods. Add up the pieces and the sugar content, then decide if you really want them all.

Increase the child's direct experience with the real world. Take children to see new places and introduce them to people of many kinds. In every town there are street fairs, local theater groups, museums, parks, parades, sporting events, libraries. When a new gas station opens up, go say hello, or when a neighbor moves in, go introduce yourself and your children. Take a bus ride, just to see what you can see. This says to the child, "The world is interesting, worth experiencing first-hand."

It is especially important to broaden the child's experience with people of many kinds. If a child knows real people who are Black, Chinese, Puerto Rican, Dutch, handicapped, elderly, or members of other minorities, he will not be so vulnerable to the stereotyped portrayals he will see on TV. Real-life experience is the best defense against televised stereotypes.

Help your whole family to experience the world through the senses and the arts. Encourage the young to paint, to dance, to play music, to sing. Make things in the kitchen, plant seeds in the garden or a windowsill pot. The idea isn't to excel at these endeavors but through them to experience the world.

Read aloud. Read a book aloud to the child every day, once at bedtime and also at another time. Nursery rhymes are excellent material to start with. Their brevity and rhyming have a great appeal to children, especially when they are repeated and repeated. Whether they are read from a book or recited from memory and embellished with finger plays or song, as children hear nursery rhymes over and over they begin to *anticipate* the words and soon they will supply the words before you say them. Thus they learn *how to remember* and acquire an ear for language.

Choose picture books and story books that interest you as well as the child, and your own interest will carry over. Take children to the library on a regular basis. (See the list of classic read-aloud books in Appendix A.)

Older children enjoy having books read aloud to them, although too often parents give up the practice as children learn to read by themselves. This is unfortunate because the child's interest in the world is often far more sophisticated than the books that he is able to read by himself in the second, third, and fourth grades.

Develop and maintain your own interest in reading. The more the child sees *you* reading adult books, the greater the chance the child will like reading.

LIMITING TV TIME

The parents who are happy with their family's use of TV often share one characteristic: They have learned one way or another how to say "no." Too often, parents who have become uneasy about kids' viewing let them do it anyway, because it seems to be easier than dealing with the friction that may result from setting limits. I think that in the long run it is easier and wiser to bear the hassles of regulating TV viewing than to carry the guilt involved with knowing that you should have but didn't. If, through permissiveness, I let my children develop a bad habit, I am, in part, responsible.

Making judgments is one way that adults protect children's health and well-being. Young children do not have the experience necessary to make judgments about certain things. I find it helpful to remind myself from time to time that *I* am the adult and therefore have a lot more experience than children. This bolsters me in making judgments that are often unpleasant to make. Sometimes it is necessary to say "no" to TV programs and TV products. One mother points out: "You have to have a really strong conviction about TV policies or else kids will talk you right out of your rules. When I say 'no' to viewing, I say it firmly and if they ask 'why not' I say 'because I said so. . . .'" She continues, "Making judgments about what my kids do is one way I communicate my values. They know where I stand."

There are less authoritarian ways to say "no." Another parent says, "I think that's an awful program—I'd rather you didn't watch it." A more passive parent says simply, "I'd rather we watch something else." Another says, "Let's see what else is on," or "Let's see what else we can do." A "preventive" method of saying "no" is to have preplanned activities. "My kids are too busy to watch TV," says one father. By whatever method, all of these parents are employing judgment and limiting TV. No matter what the family lifestyle, some children find TV more enticing and compelling than others, and sooner or later most parents need to set some limits on time spent with "the box."

Limiting TV is also an age-specific dilemma; what is appropriate for a three-year-old is not for a twelve-year-old, and vice versa. The household with many children is obviously more complicated than the family with one or two children of similar age.

Among the hundreds of parents I talked with, many pointed out that their viewing time and patterns are affected by the number of sets in the home and the placement of those sets. Coming to terms with television is a personal matter. None of us can give answers about other people's TV viewing. But what we can do is share experiences or "case histories" involving the successful structuring of home viewing. Here are some models to adapt or embellish according to your needs:

The No-TV Model. A one percent minority in the United States *chooses* not to own a TV set. "Four years ago we sailed it out the door," says Mary Rinne, in Ann Arbor, Michigan. "We're not anti-TV," says her husband, Carl. "We're just happier without it." Mary noticed that their children, Melissa and David, would be cranky after watching it for a couple of hours. "They'd stare into space and appear to be out of touch with reality. Getting them to come to supper was nearly impossible. Now they read more, play, and draw pictures. We do things together that we might not be doing if there were a TV in the house," Mary says.

"With two parents working, we have to use our time together carefully," Carl evaluates. "Our house is quieter now—we're not inundated with commercial messages, and TV doesn't interfere with our family relationships. When it's here, TV calls out and says, 'Pay attention to me.' The only voice you'll hear in our house is a human one—not the tube's."

The no-TV model is strongly advocated for children under five years old. "There are factors in a child's perceptual development which make him quite unready to take on TV viewing as a major experience while still so young. While television can be a useful resource to the older child, it is basically detrimental to the child under five or six years old," said the late Dr. Dorothy H. Cohen, professor at the Bank Street College of Education in New York.

The parent of the child under six is advised to be wary of

even the "good" programs on TV; even if there were "good" programs all day and all night, it would not be good for children to be watching them in lieu of other experiences.

The Hour-a-Day Model. The "hour-a-day" rule works for many families with young children and is recommended for children seven to eleven if they want to watch TV. When there are preschoolers in the household, the "hour" is usually allotted for viewing *Sesame Street, Captain Kangaroo,* or *Mr. Rogers'.*

The hitch is that after developing the daily TV routine at age three or four, kids move on to other channels, taking their habit with them. One mother who set up the "hour-a-day" plan a year ago says:

> For all my good intentions in permitting my four-year-old son to watch *Sesame Street,* the habit of "TV and snacks" comes easily. When Billy invites friends in after school (especially in the winter when it gets dark early) they frequently want to watch TV—*Gigantor, Batman, Spiderman.* Under the "hour-a-day" plan they would (by age five) tend to select one of these violent episodes rather than, say, *Mr. Rogers'.* My intuition tells me that this isn't a good idea—on the other hand, it's only one hour. . . .
>
> But I soon found myself spending an unreasonable amount of energy as "manager" of TV policy. Often I hear, "I should get two hours today because I missed yesterday—but [brother] John can't watch with me because he watched yesterday at Bobby's house and I didn't. . . ." Or, John wants to watch *Sesame* for "his" hour, and Billy wants to watch *Gilligan's Island* later. How shall I monitor the situation so that one boy doesn't watch both programs, thereby creating some unfairness under the present policy? As firmly as I believe that children of this age should be limited to an hour a day, I am often weary from the effort to be consistent in enforcing it. *Each day television is a negotiable issue!* The negotiations often have a negative tone—and assign to me (again) a negative function.

The Weekend-Rule Model. An increasing number of parents who do limit TV viewing of their school-age children are employing the "weekend rule." They do this for essentially two reasons: to save the week nights for homework and quiet activities, and to avoid the hassles of daily negotiations over apportioning and selecting TV viewing. A parent relates:

> One September, after a summer of outdoor activity had drawn us all from the house and the TV, Bill and I faced the fact that shorter days and daylight savings time would soon make afternoon TV viewing a question. We discussed what kind of policy might be reasonable to consider and by what process it should be developed. We agreed that the adults in the house should make these kinds of judgments about our children's education rather than giving all family members an equal vote in the matter. My husband and I were tending toward a "weekends only" plan.
>
> Later we asked each of our kids, aged 10 and 12, "What programs do you most like to see on TV?" One said, "Tennis," and the other said, "The world series." Our plan was implemented with relative ease because the children's wishes for their favorite programming—sports—can be satisfied on the weekends. Even so, there are requests for "specials" and other weekday programs to which we have to say no.
>
> As a matter of routine our portable TV goes into the attic on Sunday evening (out of sight, out of mind) and isn't in view again until after dinner on Friday. Evenings are spent practicing spelling words, etc. Our children go to bed at 8:30 or 9:00 (earlier than most of their friends) and this allows them to be well rested and well prepared for school. In the course of the weekend they usually watch a lot of sports on TV—and inevitably some other stuff which I don't care for: Six Million Dollar Man, Eye Witness News, etc. But real-life activities—soccer teams, street games, and household chores—frequently interrupt this potential weekend viewing.

Variations. The Schmidt pattern is more diffuse and flexible than the basic models already described. It allows for the individual differences in the children—Katie, fifteen; Betsy, twelve; and Peter, nine. Their mom says:

> I limit the time spent viewing by saying no TV before breakfast or after school. I rule out these times because it creates minimum friction. In the evenings and on weekends I watch over each child's viewing in a different way by encouraging certain programs and discouraging others. I present alternatives on purpose to interrupt their viewing.
>
> I think that most TV is mindless and becomes an excuse for not doing other things, but I know they will watch some. I feel that it's important to have only one set and situate it in the midst of the living area so that there will be human life flowing through the vicarious experience. I want them to have to quarrel sometimes about program choices, and compromise, and take turns. In all of this I have considerable patience but there is one thing I won't do—that is sit there with them and watch some program I can't stand, like *Love Boat*. Granted, it is sometimes important to talk about the programs, but I feel *I am more useful to them as a role model who is in the next room doing something creative* which I really love to do, rather than sitting there dutifully asking questions or making interpretations which they really don't hear very well anyway.

Occasionally at PTA meetings people say that if parents curtail TV viewing kids won't have anything to talk about in school. This is pure nonsense! TV is a popular topic—and all children talk about it sometime—but unless the child has rather serious personality problems, he or she can find many other things to talk about as well. (How many times do you have to see *Batman* in order to enter into a conversation—or to know what he does with a cape?)

Another "myth" is that if you limit TV in your home your children are likely to run away to the neighbors to watch. That's not true. Of course, they will enjoy watching sometimes, but if their home life is an active one they will not be preoccupied with running over to the neighbors' to watch.

Time limits are most necessary for the very young and may be expanded as children grow older. However, most children do watch some TV, so most parents' goals might be to develop a combination of time limits and content limits that vary according to the age and needs of the child.

Mini-Methods. Short of elaborate plans, a parent can go by "rules of thumb" which often make sense to kids. Two parents report: "We always check the newspaper to see if there's anything on that we want to watch—not just turn the set on to see which is the least objectionable program. We watch *programs*, not just television."

EVALUATING CONTENT

What is a good program for children? Cartoons? Mr. Rogers'? *Captain Kangaroo?* What about situation comedies? Game shows? Soap operas? Christmas specials? Commercials? Promotional messages? Rose Kennedy said that she carefully selected her sons' and daughters' books—mainly for educational and inspirational values, ideas, artistic designs, and illustrations. "They were never chosen hit or miss."

If young children are going to spend time with media, their parents should make judgments about its content. Nothing is more "hit or miss" than the spin of the TV dial. And sorting out the stories on television is more difficult than sorting out books. One cannot check out the TV stories by previewing them before the children see them. Only in unusual circumstances does a person get the opportunity to preview a program before its air date when it is beamed simultaneously into millions of homes. (New technologies, such as video disks and video cassettes, may change this, but for now, it's broadcast TV.) Frequently parents report that they have wanted to fly across the room in the midst of a program to hit the "off button"—but to no avail, for by then the image has been consumed.

In addition to statistical analyses there are various published lists of "good" and "bad" programs. Such lists, however, may or may not take into account *your* values or your children's needs. Inevitably, each parent must make evaluations and judgments. Here is a framework for evaluating children's programs:

1. What kind of distinction is made between what is real and make-believe? In *Mr. Rogers' Neighborhood* the transition is clearly signaled by the trolley's journey from Mr. Rogers' house to the "Neighborhood of Make-Believe" (so labeled). This is in contrast to *Bionic Woman* or *Six Million Dollar Man* in which the major characters are endowed with magical super-human powers upon which the storyline is built. The slow motion sets the bionic action off as unique but not as make-believe.

2. Is this segment geared to my child's level of understanding? Many children watch programs which were not produced for them but for adults. Situation comedy humor (underlined by a laugh track) is often based on put-down humor and sexual titillation. Children are rarely in a position to profit from such humor.

3. How are problems solved? By using others? By hitting someone? By revenge? With money? Magic? By cooperation? Determination? When Kojak and Jim Rockford skirt the law to enforce "justice," when the Bionic Man and the Incredible Hulk require superhuman strength to get out of a tight situation, when Charlie's Angels use their earthly assets to entrap their prey, they telecast a message about what is acceptable and effective in problem solving. Talking things over or thinking things through lack the action of a quick punch or a breathless chase. They are static in a medium that demands movement.

4. What role models are offered in the program? Does the portrayal suggest that women are happiest doing the dishes, while men are active and "making change"? One parent says, "I blew the whistle when I saw my daughter watching *Jeannie* use magical powers—not to improve civilization, but to please a man. She does everything for the man she calls 'Master' and is only happy when he is happy with her." Similar role

models say: be tough, buy expensive products, and so on.

5. What is the pace of this program? What are the production techniques used? How often does the picture or the camera angle change? Which special effects are employed—animation, laugh track? What is the noise level or confusion level in the audio portion? The ordinary "chase" cartoon is characterized by jumpy movements, explosions, and almost constant laugh track or noise.

6. How is humor used? To what extent does a laugh track tell the child what to laugh at—in other words, what is funny and what is not? Archie Bunker calls his son-in-law a "meat head," and uproarious laughter suggests to the child that this is funny.

7. How is the world portrayed? Is it a dangerous place, something to be feared and avoided? Or is it a wonder to be explored? Gerbner and Gross, cited earlier, showed that on TV the world is shown to be far more violent than it really is—and fear results.

8. What kind of commercials are associated with this program? Junk food? Floor wax? Radial tires? Personal hygiene products?

9. What is the response of the child to particular programs and to cumulative viewing? Is he or she cooperative or aggressive after viewing? Excitable or calm? What kinds of play follow the program? What kinds of fantasy does it inspire? What kinds of behavior had the program encouraged? What body movements? Eye movements? Hand use?

10. Is this program *good enough* to be worth my time? What if there were "good" programs on 24 hours a day? Would you watch them all?

One parent who has learned how to both limit TV time and evaluate TV content explains:

When my oldest was three or four, my husband and I used to think it was great how he'd get up on Saturday morning, get himself a drink and a piece of fruit, and watch TV for a couple of hours—allowing us the luxury of sleeping until 9:30 or 10:00. Then we noticed that when we did get up and tell him to turn off the set, we had a fight on our hands. He would complain and whine and be cranky for quite a while. We decided TV time had to be cut down. We literally pulled the plug. He complained a lot, but he never touched the plug.

Our second son has had limited access to the TV from the beginning, so he doesn't look for it as much as the older boy did (and still does, sometimes).

Sometimes we feel out of the mainstream—when he doesn't recognize all the *Sesame Street* characters in the toy store, or when he points to the exit sign and says, "Look at the numbers." (Recognizing the exit sign was one of our older boy's first academic achievements, thanks to *Sesame Street.*) I prefer to have my little one watch *Mr. Rogers'*, if anything, because it's only a half-hour long, and because I've come to feel that if he's going to learn anything from TV, I'd rather it be gentleness and a feeling of self-worth than the letter "E."

LISTENING TO THE CHILD

Even more important than watching the TV screen is listening—listening to the child. Listening may give vital clues to what the child is feeling or thinking about TV images. Rather than telling the child what TV images mean to you (an adult), let the child tell you what the messages are saying to him. (I don't think the child really knows what the images mean to him, but he can give clues about a part of that meaning. For example, a four-year-old can tell you, "I want Tootsie Pops," but cannot tell you that advertising is making him slowly cynical, because he doesn't understand that this is going on.) To learn how to listen to a child the adult should:

- Stop talking. This isn't easy. It can be observed that in groups of adults and children, usually the adults talk more and interrupt children more often than children interrupt adults.
- Appreciate the degree of difficulty in listening. It takes a lot of energy to listen, concentrate, scan, survey, store up, sort out.
- Absorb not just the child's words, but how they are said.

What disgusts, excites, or anesthetizes him? When is the child seized in attention?
- Listen with respect and dignity. Listen for what it means.
- Take time with the listening activity—this shows that you think it's worthwhile. Listen in such a way that the child sees that it's important.
- Listen to (watch) the body responses to particular images and sustained viewing.
- Watch your child to know his tolerance for tension. Be aware of your child's reaction to specific types of programs. What causes the most tension, is most agitating or stimulating?
- Understand that there might be discrepancies in what the child *says* he's taking in and what is really being registered. (While watching *Emergency*, Joshua says, "It's not scary," but he chews on the corner of his blanket, and his eyes are round as saucers.)

INTRODUCE TV AS AN EDUCATIONAL TOOL

Frequently a parent's time must be spent counteracting the images and misinformation conveyed on TV, but the alert parent can also seize opportunities to open lines of communication and educate family members in the way that they need or wish to be educated.

- TV can show positive behaviors such as thoughtfulness, helpfulness, cooperation, and sharing. Mr. Rogers' and *Sesame* try to do this.
- TV permits us to see life in a different context (*Roots*, for example) and changes our perspective by changing our vantage point. It can bring the child the moon or take him to Africa or to the bottom of the ocean.
- TV can present material to be learned by rote such as number and letter recognition (*Sesame Street*).
- TV can introduce a child to books by talking about or reading the book to children—especially with the suggestion that he go find the book at the library.
- TV can teach physical techniques in sports or dance or handicrafts which can then be imitated.

- TV can serve as a springboard to family discussion about social issues such as racism, drugs, or sexuality, which might otherwise not occur. *My Mom Is Having a Baby,* an ABC Afterschool Special, won wide acclaim from parents.
- TV can help to solve some of the parenting problems it has helped to create. It can, for example, teach parents how to be a model for imaginative play in the ways mentioned earlier. It can *show* parents in the act of saying "no" to their children in loving and creative ways that can be adapted by parents at home. For this, TV would work better than a book.

When parents choose to turn on the TV to watch a specific program for a specific reason, they are using TV constructively as a learning tool. But programs must be selected very carefully. Parents must always consider their child's level of understanding and remember that even a good thing can be overdone.

DISCUSSING THE CONTENT OF TV

Watching TV along with children can yield important awareness for the parent. To some (minor) degree it can mitigate the negative effects of TV and to a greater degree it can extend the positive effects of TV. When parents use TV as a springboard to family communication and when they help the child to *make connections* between ideas and images, they are participating creatively in the education of the young.

A young Black woman speaks of her observation of her five-year-old son. She says:

> Selective and controlled viewing are not enough to subvert some of the more "deadly" messages about minorities being conveyed on television. Parent–child discussion has proven most effective for me. Despite limitations in his ability to understand certain television content due to his age, talking to my son about minority characters and situations on TV help him to understand what's happening, and helps me to understand what he is seeing. In one incident, for example, where Fred Sanford rants and raves

about how ugly Aunt Esther is on *Sanford and Son*, I noticed how intently he was watching. "Do you think he looks like Grandpa?" I asked.

"Yep," he replied.

"Do you think Grandpa ever acts like that?" I then asked.

"No, Mommy, Grandpa's not on TV," he explained. Immediately following the show, we talked about the difference between how people on television act and how people that we know in real life act. I doubt that his five-year-old mind understood everything we discussed, but I view this discussion as a continuous and cumulative process. More than anything else, "Mommy's TV control" involves communication with my child, talk and more talk, knowing what he's feeling and thinking while he's watching, indicating related situations with minorities in real life, and pointing out the nonstereotyped examples of minorities on TV where they occur. For example, we searched several superhero programs on Saturday morning one week, looking for a Black superhero. When we finally found two, "Superstretch" and "Microwoman," we were both excited. While I wasn't exactly ecstatic about the characters themselves, I felt rewarded when my son explained to me, "See, Mommy, superheroes come in all colors!"[1]

Racial and ethnic minorities have some of the toughest situations to "talk out" because television is so full of disadvantageous portrayals of them. Black children see mostly whites on TV; Jewish children see only Christmas on TV and never a Jewish holiday; the handicapped child sees mainly very active, attractive children on TV; and of course the elderly see youth. Talking about these exclusions can help, though I'm not confident that it helps very much. In these cases, it seems to me, the parent cannot explain away what is inadequate in the TV portrayal, but he or she might use the situation as a springboard to make comparisons with real life or feelings or related situations which have meaning to the child. The fact that the adult cared enough to spend the time and talk (about anything) with the child must count for something and contribute positively to the child's feeling about him or herself.

Some more general kinds of content affect everybody—sexuality, violence, and advertising are with us constantly on TV and need to be discussed more.

Talking about violence in real life as well as on TV is important. Consider using these kinds of questions as "starters": How did you feel when you saw that? Have you ever seen that in real life? Why do you suppose that person did that? Can you think of another way he could have solved that problem? Also talk about violence and how it hurts. Talk about anything in the program that might have upset the child. If the child wakes up in the night with a nightmare (possibly stimulated by TV viewing), there is probably nothing to talk about right then as the child is too irrational and upset. Hold the child—for a long time if necessary, until he or she is relaxed and secure enough to go back to sleep.

Talking about advertising can be useful for the child who is over eight or nine. You can teach that the intent of the ad is to make you buy something. You can point out the techniques used in producing the ad, such as the use of catchy songs, movie stars, sexual nuance. If the ad promises to solve a problem, identify the problem and how the ad claims to provide answers. Talk about TV foods that can cause cavities and TV toys that may break too soon. None of this will help the younger child, but some of this kind of conversation will get through to the older child.

A study prepared for the Canadian Radio–TV Telecommunications Commission noted that televised portrayals of family life offer parents and children opportunities to "talk about topics they would otherwise probably not discuss." Children said that they would like to fashion their family life after what they see on TV. The report said, "Communication and shared activity are the most sought-after experiences of youth with parents. They are actions always perceived and admired in TV families." Family members, therefore, might ask each other: What have we done as a family that would make interesting stories for TV? If we couldn't play ourselves, what actors would we select for the parts? Why? Do TV families deal with the same kinds of problems we do? How much is our family like the TV families? If watching TV is so popular, why don't we see families on TV watching TV?

Talking about TV is helpful. But as an antidote for poor programming, it is a limited remedy. Parents trying to learn to live with TV in these various ways are apt to feel lonely, burdened, and very frustrated. It is hard to set limits on products and programs that are beamed to kids on TV. It is difficult to assimilate all this new children's material well enough to listen and talk about it with sensitivity. Parents need help from each other, from neighbors, babysitters, grandparents—and from broadcasters who are responsible for the programming.

The parent who is home all day especially needs help. This parent has the constant responsibility of saying "no" while the parent who may be away working can arrive home in the evening for dinner, fun, and games.

But one cannot just kick the set and give up in exasperation. Joining a parent-support group (or starting one) is one constructive move. Action for Children's Television, a national group, and its local affiliates, provide models of how it has been done in some places. It is helpful to be in touch with others who are trying to cope wisely with television. Just finding other people who worry and care about the same things you do can give a parent new energy. Together you can share ideas, communicate your ideas to the local schools, and perhaps become involved in communications issues as they affect the whole society.

The central question is one of protection for the young. How do we protect the inner environment of children? In our technological society, the first wave of outrage has been against what's happening to our outer environment. It is and will be even harder to defend and protect the inner environment, but we can begin by regulating the technology of the outer environment.

Too much "care-taking" has been given over to machines. The children of Telstar need more human, adult care-givers at home, in school—and beyond.

▪ 9 ▪
ACTION
IN
SCHOOL

If educators are out of touch
with television, they are out of touch with
an important force in people's lives.
And if there's a crisis in education,
it comes partly from the fact that
educators don't recognize that
they're not dealing with Gutenberg people,
but a whole new race of television people.

Les Brown, television correspondent
The New York Times

The new race of television people has landed in school. Raised on the language of pictures, not words, these children have new and different kinds of capacities—some of which we can't even describe yet. The world of picture media has created new needs in these children, so that new skills are required to teach them.

The purpose of this chapter is to ask specifically how schools can address the needs of the child who is growing up on television. "Anything which equips students to deal with the barrage of information beamed at them by TV is a valid part of the curriculum. We should define *understanding media* as a basic skill, identify the component parts of the skill and then discover how to teach them," says Dr. Calvert Schlick, superintendent of instructional services for the Mamaroneck (New York) Public Schools.

Television has changed the world much more than it has changed children's classrooms. Suddenly there's more forward information outside the classroom than in it, as instant replay and satellite interconnection become commonplace in everybody's living room.

By the time a child comes to kindergarten he has logged thousands of hours of TV, a fact which the curriculum has invariably failed to take into account. Now more people watch movies and TV shows than read books; they get more of their news from television than they do from newspapers and magazines. By high school graduation, most students will have spent 18,000 hours with the "television curriculum" but only 12,000 hours with the school curriculum. Whether we consider visual media inferior, superior, or equal to print, these conditions are a given. Our educators have a responsibility to develop skills in students that will help them to deal critically with the great input of visual information. It is time for our educators to adapt themselves to these new circumstances.

It is possible for future generations to be proficient in reading, writing, and arithmetic as well as in understanding all media. But then we must expand the scope and design of the school curriculum. Toward this goal, there are some first steps that schools can take:

- Acknowledge the special needs of "TV children."
- Increase the direct experiences of children, especially those which involve use of hands and whole body.
- Consider appropriate in-school viewing of TV.
- Teach critical viewing skills, particularly in upper grades.
- Teach use of television as a process tool and relate this to the use of all art/media.
- Rediscover reading, writing, listening skills.
- Help the young to deal with the accumulated misinformation from TV.
- Work with parents in reducing mindless viewing levels at home.

What should result is an art/media skills program connected to all curriculum areas. Media skills should be organized, sequenced, and keyed to the various developmental stages. For example, is it possible the use of instamatic cameras by children will develop their perceptual capacities and/or reason? If so, how? And when would be the best time to begin such activities with children in terms of their developmental abilities and their other media skills? Should this activity be deferred until the child is "rooted" in reading? Why, or why not? Likewise, at which point(s) can cassette tape recorders serve particular developmental needs? Likewise other media: dance, fingerpaint, sand, water, film or video tape production?

There should be a time line and an order to the teaching of all media. In terms of the child's perceptual development, there is a "prime time" for introducing paint, print, clay, film, television production, etc.

SPECIAL NEEDS

Teachers who have taught for many years and have known large groups of children across generations see today's young as a "new breed." They recognize peculiarities that the parent with one child or the new teacher with her first class can't perceive. Teachers with 15 or more years of experience say that today's children come to school with stunning pieces of information, but that this knowledge is largely unintegrated and unusable; the children have a shorter attention span, poor listening skills, and difficulty in following verbal directions.

"We see both more passivity and more frenzied behavior," says one.

"They are waiting to be told," says another. "They're not motivated because they're so used to being entertained."

Others say, "Nothing comes from inside," noting a decline in many children's ability to concentrate, to play imaginatively, and to relate to others. "They expect everything to happen instantly." (See Chapter 3, "The Effects on Learning and Perception," and Chapter 4, "The Effects on Reading.")

Habitual television viewing promotes this behavior by conditioning the "inner environment" of the young child, immobilizing the hands and eyes. New calm, strength, and integration in the child would be produced by school programs which invite involvement of the whole body and all the senses via direct experience, especially involvement in the arts and basic, organized, repetitive teaching of reading, writing, and arithmetic. This kind of high level of participation will promote what Marshall McLuhan called the "balanced sensorium": stable personalities and fuller learners. From this base, a person is in a position to benefit from the miracles that television may offer. But we aren't helping ourselves to that position by ignoring the schools of today; these are just the programs now being slashed from school life by voters who do not understand that these activities provide an essential balance to the massive TV addiction of the modern child.

INCREASE DIRECT EXPERIENCE

The role of the school and the function of the teacher are changing, chiefly because *the preschool child's ratio of vicarious experience to direct experience is now very high,* in sharp contrast to one short generation ago. Now, from birth, all sorts of information are indiscriminately beamed at the passive child. What is sharply reduced or absent is the base of *direct* experience in the preschool years which would help the child to integrate this vicarious "experience."

What the school can do is create socializing experiences to help the child integrate helter-skelter information and make meaning from it all. More "learning by doing" and direct experience in school life will help to balance the excessive vicarious experience of today's preschooler when he arrives in kindergarten. This balancing of experience will promote the health of mind and body, and hence all learning.

To create a counterculture of direct experience, the school should ask itself: What are the materials that make life "easy"—and then throw them out! Out with the pseudo-experience of kits, ditto sheets, workbooks, premixed paint, boxes of machine-cut shapes (the round, orange pumpkins with triangle eyes, etc.). Free of all this, more attention can be given to the things that require children to exert some real effort: paper scrap, cooking equipment, woodworking bench, paint, puppets, cones, hoops, dress-up materials, sandpaper, wheelbarrow, simple binoculars, balls of all sizes, growing plants and trees. (See the full list in Appendix B.) These materials invite children to engage pent-up energies accumulated in too much passive watching and ask the child to develop ideas from *inside out*, by *doing*. They can learn from cooking, stacking, sorting, building, dancing, hammering, sawing, planting seeds. Stringing beads, an activity scoffed at by nouveau educators, offers the child a chance to develop small muscles in the hands—likewise cut-and-paste activities. In fact, these activities are so useful as eye–hand coordination exercises that they are employed as a basic part of some remedial reading therapies. How ironic that what was once simple child's play is now a part of expensive therapy! These "ordinary" direct experiences are instrumental in promoting later cognitive learning.

But the teacher who would teach in this way might not meet with instant understanding, and adult visitors to the kindergarten will overlook much of the vital action. An intuitive teacher explains the importance of painting for her five- and six-year-olds:

> There's a great deal going on in that painting session. First, we always mix our own paint. The child will learn after doing for some days that four teaspoons of powdered paint and a half-measure of water will make paint of a nice consistency. Each will select colors, size of paper, size of brush and begin. I don't watch what's being painted as much as I watch the painter. I try not to ask, "What is it?" or "Tell me about it." I might say, "I like it." I try to ask myself, "What does the child need to learn at that moment?" You make a thing go a little faster if you can introduce something or encourage something. I want *them* to make judgments, to find similarities, to think up and execute an idea, to use resources outside the classroom—not just books, but people and all they know. *So I watch the painter carefully.*

She continues:

Today Jimmy's painting looked like a soggy mess—a big
ball of paint all round and dripping. The colors came at
you all at once. But that painting session had involved a
well-thought drama which only Jimmy and I know. In the
beginning the car was going down the road, but it met
another car and there was a great crash with many circles
and different colors of paint. The hopes and plans and
feelings and so on might not have been visible in that ball
of "yukky" paint which probably had a hole in the middle
(where the crash was). Nobody else could see the colors,
sizes, shapes and judgments. (Which colors should I use?
Which brush? What comes next? etc.) When the picture is
finished there is more to think about: What shall we do
with it? Shall we ask the others to come and see? Shall we
hang it up? Where? Inside the classroom? Outside? Down
the hall by brother's room? How high? Is it level?

School administrators sometimes miss the point, as they look
for "results," scores, and tidiness. One second-grade teacher
complained, "There are fifty kids in here each day—working!
But the principal doesn't know how to interpret what he sees."
She offers an illustration:

Today the children went out to haul in an old limb that
had fallen off a tree in the wind. All day they were busily
sawing and sorting and stacking the bark in bundles of
ten. They think they're going to sell it around the school.
When the principal stopped in I explained this and asked,
"If they come to you, will you buy some?" He said, "Well,
no, I don't have a fireplace."

Broadened experience would balance the senses of the visually overextended child who needs to use his ears, hands, and
whole body more. By age eleven, the child with many different
kinds of experience in many arts and media will bring to the
TV screen a natural interpreting ability; this can be brilliantly
extended by two forms of school training: the teaching of
critical viewing skills and hands-on TV production.

IN-SCHOOL TV

School television will come of age—it's already growing rapidly. In New York, Channel 13 (PBS) beams 30 hours a week of programming meant for school use: *The Draw Man, Think About, Let's All Sing, The World of B. J. Vibes, All About You, Freestyle, Guten Tag in Deutschland, Survival Skills for the Classroom Teacher, Cover to Cover, The Electric Company, Sesame Street, Juba, The Word Shop, Word Smith, Math Patrol, The Metric System, About Animals, Search for Science, What's in the News, The World Wars*, to name a few.

Teachers in the schools reached by these programs no longer fear (as they might have 15 years ago) that their jobs will be lost to the "TV teacher"; rather, many have befriended TV and even returned to college to gain skills in becoming "all-media" educators. Some school systems have created jobs for a "TV coordinator" to teach staff and students how to use TV, to develop curriculum, and to report to parents about this important force in children's lives. Upper and lower schools are using broadcast, cable, and closed-circuit TV to provide basic services for the following kinds of reasons:

- To extend superior teaching to a greater number of students. "We need a political science course and consultants for our teachers," says the principal of a K–12 school in the U.S. Virgin Islands. It is better to be able to present an "A+" teacher on video tape than to omit the course offering because of lack of a qualified instructor. Even in very small schools or remote areas a skilled discussion leader can be found to help students interact with the film or video tape, thus extending superior teaching to those who might not otherwise have the benefit of it. There is a scarcity of good science teaching in the United States; in fact most elementary students receive inadequate science education. The few good science teachers could be shared with millions of students if they taught via TV. Further, science experiments around which concept teaching should be based are well done by camera close-up shots that enable children to see them better than in "real life." TV becomes a superior teacher whenever it is required that you *show* something rather than *tell* it.

- To bring to the classroom material that hasn't been a part of the curriculum. Until *Roots* was watched in 36 million homes, Black heritage was not a subject in most schools. Now more than 250 colleges and universities offer courses based on the film and book; numerous high schools incorporate the series in history teaching, some of them taping it off the air for class use; and some elementary schools assign the series as homework to be viewed at home.

- To provide a retrieval system (via video tape) for previously telecast material which may supplement the regular curriculum. Many schools are using video cassette recorders to tape off-the-air programs which tie in with teaching objectives in the school curriculum. For example, the first moon walk was telecast at midnight but was reshown the next day in schools where it had been taped.

- To facilitate "in-house" communication. Some large schools are wired for closed circuit (CCTV) and use the system to convey basic school news and messages—to share student endeavors and dramatic productions. A new school nurse may be introduced to the students in a personal way on TV, a fire drill procedure explained, a "thank you" offered, etc.

- To capture the interest of students who are slow in using print media or who may be functionally illiterate. When other methods seem to be unsuccessful, the phlegmatic students will discuss or even write about TV programs. They *can* be reached, one way or another. TV will increase the proliferation of visual material in the schools. Equal effort and interest should be invested in developing critical viewing skills in the consumers of this material.

DEVELOP CRITICAL VIEWING SKILLS

Critical viewing skills are an extension of critical thinking skills. The goal should be to develop a mentally active viewer, one who does not merely soak up TV's outpourings but who can process these as well. Just as the term "print literacy" refers to the ability to read and write words, "visual literacy" refers to the ability to understand and use picture media. Most frequently, the term "visual literacy" means interpreting TV, although film and magazine ads may be included. Critical viewing skills are needed as a defense against victimization by the cumulative power of the TV medium's effects.

What are these skills? They include:

- The ability to evaluate and manage one's own television viewing behavior. For many people, TV viewing occurs almost unconsciously rather than as a result of deliberate and active decision making. A discriminating viewer chooses whether, when, and what to watch. He watches programs, not just "television." Informed choice is also guided by a knowledge of the potential effects of TV viewing.
- A knowledge of the business of television. Students need to learn to question what they see on television in terms of how it got there, why, and what it means. To develop this skill, they need to know how television programs are planned and produced and to examine the images and messages that are presented. Armed with sufficient knowledge of how television operates and with practice in questioning what they see on television, students will learn that television's reality can indeed be questioned and examined.
- The ability to recognize when manipulative arguments and strategies are employed. Visual and auditory messages can be analyzed in terms of structure and validity of content. In doing so, students can identify persuasive techniques, analyze values, and clarify their own values in relation to the TV messages.
- The ability to evaluate artistic and technical elements of programming. The aware viewer should understand character, plot, casting. He or she should understand how the pace, camera angles, and audio accompani-

ments affect the perception of character, theme, and so on.
- The ability to recognize effects of TV viewing. By becoming aware of potential effects of TV, students can learn to manage them or avoid them.

Eventually, the new media literates should study short films and TV programs, examining plot, characters, setting, and theme, as well as the techniques employed. The more sophisticated students may even study the history of television and the "business behind the box." Above all, the literate person should be able to make rational judgments about the medium. But in television, as in any medium, there are levels to literacy and many steps to critical viewing skill.

It would be a serious misplacement of energy to spend much time in the early elementary grades in direct pursuit of these skills. Developmental limitations in early and middle childhood strongly recommend that analytic and evaluative abilities be developed via other art media and lower levels of technology before turning to TV. It is silly to expect, as some curriculum writers do, that the child viewer should be able to understand the psychological implications of commercials, distinguish fact from fiction, recognize and appreciate differing and opposing views, and develop an understanding of the style and content of dramatic presentations, documentaries, public affairs, news, and other programming.

It is a misuse of time for a kindergarten or first-grade teacher to spend a significant part of the school day trying to teach six-year-olds how to differentiate fantasy from reality on TV. Developmentally, they are not apt to be able to do it. Better let the six-year-old paint and be lost in the fantasy in that activity, or let him chat, run, or read. Teaching of critical viewing skills could be productive starting at about grade four, when the child's perceptual development can accommodate such teaching. Until fourth grade, however, there are other ways to demonstrate the significance of television programs in the child's life.

TV AS COMMON EXPERIENCE

Skillful teachers try to build on a child's experience. Because TV viewing takes up so large a portion of a child's time, and because children in the same age group generally see the same programs, some teachers try to build on the children's common experience in TV viewing in order to carry their interest into other subjects. Rosemary Potter, a Florida first-grade teacher, began developing teaching games or strategies that would utilize TV as "shared experience." When Ms. Potter first raised the subject of TV in class discussion it brought forth gleeful rapport, large group attention, and high motivation. Yet, she said, "All I had done was to ask children to tell me about commercial television."

She had asked each pupil to tell the name of his or her favorite show—and made a list on the blackboard, and then developed "The Thinking Game," in which a child secretly selected a TV title and offered the class a "clue" to the setting, plot, or characters of that program. "I was astounded by the stored knowledge which the children possessed about television as shown by their detailed guessing, explanations and clues," Potter said.

One hitch in this method is that at some point adults need to be able to respond to children's conversation about TV shows; they need to know what those shows are about. Some teachers consider it their homework to check out Saturday-morning cartoons—*Jeannie*, *Gilligan*, *Godzilla*, *Gigantor*, and the current prime-time action thriller. Knowing about the shows gives teachers clues to the imagery children bring to class, and this makes them more active listeners. (Someone should compile a basic guide to the programs children watch most. The guide would tell what the shows are, what the emphasis of each is, who the characters are, and something about their usual behaviors.)

In her book, *New Season: The Positive Use of Commercial Television with Children*, Rosemary Potter explains hundreds of games that utilize TV data to teach basic skills, games with names like "Alpha Order," "B for Batman," "Cartoon Comp," "Context Cue," "Word Banker," "Why Name . . . ," and others. She says:

> I first asked children to name their favorite programs, telling them I would make a book listing them. This would be a book for them to read, discuss, and illustrate. I asked them how we would remember where each program was listed in the large looseleaf book we would make. We listened to all the suggestions offered . . . and the possibilities and difficulties of numbering and random entering.
>
> I then suggested that the children examine the idea that the programs be listed by their first letters matched to the alphabet chart they already know. . . . After a few days of Alpha Order practice in this TV-related fashion, most of the class could help make accurate Alpha Order decisions.[1]

Aa	Bb	Dd
Addams Family	Bugs Bunny	Devlin
Adventures of Gilligan	Bob Newhart	Doctors
Adam-12	Bewitched	
All in the Family	Born Free	
Apple's Way		

These exercises capitalize on children's natural interest in TV—and turn it around—to focus on print.

Other activities prompt children to confront the TV experience more directly. Kids in upper grades are asked to keep journals of viewing or other activities, to study the music in a commercial, to test out TV toys, to compare TV episodes with real life.

In one sixth grade a teacher asked: "How many of you would like to watch *All in the Family* now?" and then reviewed questions for them to keep in mind while watching a ten-minute slice of the show: Does the setting reveal something about the characters? What time of year is it? How do the characters look? How do they act? Are there conflicts between them? How do you know? Is the time involved real time? Or compressed time?

The children's responses revealed considerable insight. The Bunkers home and furnishings told them that the couple from Queens was "not rich." They correctly read Edith's mood as "upset," "furious," and "disappointed because she thought they weren't treating women equal to men." They knew that the show's action took place in the afternoon, reasoning: Edith had told the banker that she had watched a soap opera earlier on TV. "Everyone knows that soap operas don't begin until noon!" announced one boy.

Then the teacher asked the sixth-graders to concoct an ending for the episode and to "play director" by casting friends and relatives in the various *All in the Family* roles. "That was cool," said one student.[2]

About the time young people are ready to "read" video, they can also learn to "write" in the medium. They can use television as a tool rather than just see what others have made with that instrument.

TV AS A TOOL

Educators are beginning to recognize that today's child is different because of his exposure to radio, TV, movies, tapes, photography, advertising, and graphic images. Because every child is bombarded and manipulated by modern methods of mass communication, he should learn how to evaluate what he sees and hears and how to use and understand media as a form of communication. First he needs to know the mechanics of media, just as he learns the ABC's before reading and writing. If a child can create images and tape as alternate forms of communications, if he can develop film and edit and select, if he can learn to acquire (efficiently) information from nonprint material, he will be tuned into his culture in a creative and critical way. The person who is literate in any medium will know how to read and write in that medium; media making is another dimension of media consumption.

A program in visual literacy would develop students who can read and write (produce as well as consume), employing the "grammar" of video language. Ideally, by high school they would know how to use camera movement (pans, dollies, zooms, arcs), transitional devices (cuts, dissolves, wipes), structural patterns (parallel action, cross-cutting), and recognize symbols and imagery. (This is analogous to learning how to use prepositional phrases or commas while mastering print language.)

People learn to understand media by using media. Children who are using television as a tool sometimes begin in the elementary school where equipment and materials have been improvised, collected, borrowed, or made from scratch. Students in the Mamaroneck (New York) school system are prepared for a lifetime of media use through graduated exercises in media and art. At one of the community's four elementary schools, fifth- and sixth-grade kids—aged ten and eleven—operate a television station from a studio in the school's basement. With three portable cameras and a Sony video tape recorder, the youngsters present a daily newscast at 8:30 each weekday morning. *Read Me a Story,* in which a first-grader reads a story he or she has mastered, and *Studio Five,* in which fifth-graders present science experiments, are other regular features of the school station. A father, a newspaper correspondent, who visited the kids' studio observed:

> A handful of children supervised by a volunteer parent were operating sophisticated equipment and coordinating television communications as casually as we used to draw pictures in art period. Watching them, I was impressed by the absence of awe. For countless generations, children were raised on paste pots and crayons; now electronics is part of basic education, and, what's more, is regarded as a fairly commonplace tool. All to the good.[3]

The goal of this pioneering system in Mamaroneck is not merely to teach children to use TV but to use all media via involvement with all the arts and many forms of technology. In these schools, you might observe the following kinds of activities as a workup to complicated hands-on TV production. Art/media education starts in the kindergarten, where much sensory development occurs in play with nonelectric media: paint, clay, sand, water, dance, rhythms, and the scrap-building that is so basic to the child.

Electronic media for kindergarten and first grade includes records and players with earphones, filmstrips, and tapes of children's classics, films, videotapes (used sparingly). Teachers use headphones and records to structure concentration and stretch attention span, pointing out that the absence of a visual aspect forces the imagination to work. The cassette tape recorder is often used for storytelling. A first-grade teacher uses films to inspire children to new and direct art experiences. She says that a film demonstrating experiments with wet clay prompted children to imitate—and go beyond—what was shown on the film (a clear case of "modeling"). "I couldn't have demonstrated to them all that they saw on the film, but I provided opportunities to go beyond vicarious experience," she says.

A second grade is developing concepts about light and dark, basic to future study of photography and TV (as well as biology, medicine, etc.). In a darkened room with an overhead projector and about ten children, the teacher asks, "What does light go through?" Windows, glass, cellophane, air, water, a moth's wings. (In a later lesson slides were made to verify what is or is not translucent.) "Is anybody afraid of the dark?" the teacher said. (No.) "How could we make it dark?" (Eliminate light.) She turns on the overhead projector as light source, aiming it toward one wall. "Can anyone make the shadow move? Dance? Be still?" (They all try, in marvelous body movements.) "Can you make the shadows get larger? Get smaller?" (They do it.) "How could you make the shadow go away?" (One boy tries to flatten himself into the carpet, but another girl says, "Woops, we still see a little flat shadow!") "What else can you say about shadows?" the teacher asks. (They enjoy telling about experiences with shadows, fears, etc.) They continue to experiment by putting objects on the overhead projector to make shadows. To conclude the lesson, the overhead projector is turned off and the regular lights are turned on, and the teacher reads "I Have a Little Shadow that Goes In and Out with Me."

The middle grades at Mamaroneck are learning ways to tell stories with pictures. Throughout the year they will have regular, short, graduated exercises: making pinhole cameras, shooting with Instamatic cameras, developing film, making contact prints, creating "cameraless" slides. In preparation for work with moving pictures, they learn "storyboarding" and develop speaking/listening skills by using the cassette tape recorder for story-telling and interviewing. "This is appropriate technology for this age group—and using these tools is important to the next steps in understanding media," says the teacher.

Fifth-graders begin using the school's TV studio as active television producers. They learn the "first rule of the studio": Don't touch anything you haven't been trained to use. But in a short while each has been trained to use cameras, lighting systems, sound systems, the special effects panel. They like the lingo: pan, dolly, scoop, fade, super, cut. They learn how to write a script, to interview "on-camera," to organize visuals.

Sixth-graders at the Murray Avenue School all see them-selves as executive producers—managing all aspects of three-camera production. On my first trip to that studio (1968) I suppose I looked like Alice in Wonderland. Peeking through the door (with the tiny red light), I saw a busy bunch of fifth- and sixth-graders working ardently among tape decks, cam-eras, scoop lights, spotlights, and a flashing console. Pushing buttons rapidly on something that looked like the panel of an aircraft, the kids switched pictures on three monitors, taking directions from the student director who wore headphones (and braces). "Camera one, zoom in . . . music up . . ." There was no awe or awkwardness (except in me)—these kids were simply getting ready to present a daily newscast to the wired classrooms in their school at 8:30 A.M. After the news, visitors could see the production of such programs as

- *Studio Five,* a program in which fifth-graders present science experiments in uniquely visual ways.

- *Read Me A Story*, in which first graders (each one may have a turn) read a short story on-camera after rehearsing it many times, drawing a title card, planning the props, etc.
- Interview "Community Helpers," such as fire chief, school board members, local authors and artists.
- Specials such as a student-created operetta and a dramatic review and report of the sixth grade's class trip to Washington, D.C.

Mamaroneck is unique in its facilities and support for media work; its schools have more collective experience in media education than any other in the country—or perhaps the world. In the high school the student may elect the Performing Arts Curriculum Education (PACE) program which centers on experience in dance, music, theater, film, radio, and TV production. The students in these programs are indeed more critical performers, producers, and, inevitably, more critical viewers.

Dr. Calvert E. Schlick, Mamaroneck's superintendent for instructional services, is a strong believer in the arts and struggles daily to keep his schools from giving up any part of the impressive program that exists. "But I can't talk too much locally about what we do or there will be an outcry from people who don't understand that the arts (electric or non-electric) are basic—not frills."

REDISCOVERING READING

It is sometimes important to rediscover the past for new reasons. Railroads went out of use for a while when people gained easy access to auto and air travel, but now we are rediscovering railroads for the sake of the environment and energy savings. Reading, having lost ground to the easy-come entertainment of TV, should also be rediscovered for reasons of promoting the logical thinking, attention span, and training reflection or inner picture making that is clearly missing from the television experience. And reading is highly associated with success in school and in life.

Reformers are recommending remedies as farfetched as

rewriting the alphabet and/or teaching reading by watching television. The rationale for each of these ideas is interesting, although I am doubtful that either will succeed. Meanwhile, there are solid (well-tested) procedures that can be prescribed to increase pleasures with books and the ability to read:

- Teachers should read aloud to children at school (and encourage the practice at home) from a young age and for as long as possible. There is a well-established correlation between children who are read to and those who read well.
- For the young child, read nursery rhymes repeatedly and encourage *memorization* by including songs or games.
- Teachers should encourage parents to read more in front of their children and should do so themselves. Children learn by example.
- Teachers should read books aloud in class. Jean Fritz, an author and librarian, goes into the schools in her community to talk about books, titles, and enticing episodes in the stories. She says that children respond eagerly to books but that rarely does anyone *talk to them* about specific books.
- Plan structured reading times (ten minutes or more per reading) four times a day when everybody reads something—including the teacher and principal. At the Good Hope School, St. Croix, U.S. Virgin Islands, the entire student body (K–12) has four ten-minute periods a day in which everybody in the school (including the nurse and the headmaster) are reading. Proficiency has zoomed.
- Encourage students and parents to see that the daily time with books equals time spent with TV. (Tough assignment)
- Encourage listening to radio drama (if you can find it) to promote inner picture making; or employ audio tape as in-school exercise to stretch the attention span.

DEALING WITH TV'S MISINFORMATION

Much of what kids learn from TV does them a distinct disservice. They learn about sexuality in exploitive, put-down terms rather than receiving positive information about how to develop healthy, realistic relationships with oneself and with others. While neither parents nor schools have been able to provide necessary sexual education, young people have continued to take negative messages from the TV screen. While teen-age pregnancy and other sexual problems are on the rise, schools still fear controversy over introducing basic sex education. The situation invites sex education via television—perhaps on cassettes for in-school use or on cable for at-home viewing. Someone, somehow, should balance the view of sexuality that is being broadcast to the child by sitcoms and soaps.

Nutrition information dispensed by TV is hazardous to health. (See Chapter 6, "The Effects on Health and Life-style.") The typical child, seeing 400 commercials a week—mostly for sugared foods—is apt to develop snacking habits and sugar addiction, cavities, heightened tendency toward hyperactivity, and hypoglycemia; and he will bring all these effects to school. Teachers know that a poorly nourished child is less teachable than a well-nourished one.

To counter the TV commercials that kids grow up on, schools should assertively and regularly teach nutrition as part of the school curriculum.

To support good nutrition habits, schools should

- Eliminate mid-morning snacking on junk foods. If there are to be snacks at all, they should be fruits, nuts, milk, or other high-protein foods.
- Eliminate candy vending machines.
- Remove TV sets from lunchrooms where they merely reinforce or encourage the "eat with TV" habit.
- Teach all children about natural foods, basic food groups, calories, meal planning, cooking, and the importance of physical exercise.

PARENTS AND TEACHERS TOGETHER

Some schools have pressed parents to increase children's direct experience by reducing the *time* spent with television.

The Board of Education in Niagara Falls, New York, unanimously adopted a resolution urging parents and students to watch fewer programs and to select them more carefully "so that pupils will make the best possible use of their time and talents."

Some schools suggest specific time limits. At the Princeton Day School, in Princeton, New Jersey, the staff distributed to the entire parent body a staff-prepared report on the effects of television which read, in part:

> The entire Lower School Faculty is increasingly concerned with the role of television in the lives of your children and with the associated negative effects which we have observed. We remain committed to your rights as parents to determine the activities of your children outside of school, but we feel compelled to suggest some ways you can and should control your children's use of television.

The letter recommended that parents set time and content limits on TV viewing and talk to their children about the TV that they do watch.

The Kimberton Farms School near Phoenixville, Pennsylvania, asked that parents ban all TV viewing by children in nursery school, kindergarten, and first grade and that they keep children in grades 2 to 12 away from the set from Sunday night through Thursday night.

The New York Council on Children's Television has worked with many schools to increase TV awareness in parents and teachers. It recommends a four-point plan for PTA meetings:

1. The school should assign two or three basic books on children and television to be studied by staff and parents. (See "Recommended Sources," pp. 223–225.)
2. Several parents and several teachers should design a questionnaire about TV habits and viewing—what is watched, how much, where the sets are located, etc. Encourage families to complete the survey.
3. From the school-wide survey, ascertain which programs are most popular or most frequently watched.

Appoint a committee of parents and teachers to monitor these programs for a period of time, studying
values, language, specific behaviors, role models, etc.
4. Call the entire staff and parent body together for a
general meeting at which the committee presents its
findings, teachers and parents present information, and
perhaps a guest such as a child psychiatrist or community activist adds research and additional perspective.

HOPE FOR THE FUTURE

There are forces at work to strip the schools of media study,
art, music, and physical education—the very activities that put
people in touch with their senses and help them to integrate
information. One of the possibilities of the future is that
television itself will teach skills in media, art, music, and
physical education in schools and at home. It could teach
about nutrition, sexuality, basic education, and parenting. The
Chinese are using TV to teach foreign languages and work
skills. They say that their "TV College" is their most exciting
new communications project, one which aims to bring basic
education to the masses who might not otherwise have this
opportunity.

The Open University (O.U.) in Great Britain is an independent, degree-granting institution operated in conjunction with
the British Broadcasting Corporation. More than 50,000 people
in that country pay tuition for home enrollment and select
from more than 80 courses which are specially produced and
which utilize BBC radio and TV. The productions, covering
about 55 daytime hours per week for 35 weeks of the year, are
subsidized by the government.

We could develop a similar project, perhaps on a noncredit
basis, to help people learn the things they want to know. Most
parents would like to have greater access to the thoughts of
psychiatrists, pediatricians, teachers of all kinds. One TV
offering could teach people how to be good parents. An
ongoing offering could be a "talk show" about living sensibly

with children and television which could play out all of the topics discussed in this book, from the facts about eye movements to the methods of evaluating children's programs. Parents like to know what other parents are thinking and doing.

Viewed as an educational institution, TV could take everybody to the FTC hearings on sugar foods and children's advertising by televising those hearings. It can, of course, bring us sports, dance, the moon, and the floor of the sea.

John Culkin, director of the Center for Understanding Media, in New York, has said: "People who live on water should learn how to swim. People who spend a great deal of time watching television should learn how it works because it has daily access to their minds, emotions and values."

Through careful thought and instruction the "new race of television people" can learn to master the use of TV technology which so powerfully conditions them. But because this is a complex task that requires a great deal of experience, the younger children have a special need for some educational protection from the various influences of television.

▪10▪
PUBLIC
ACTION

This instrument can teach,
it can illuminate;
yes, and it can do so only
to the extent that
humans are determined
to use it to those ends.
Otherwise, it is merely lights
and wires in a box.

Edward R. Murrow
CBS News

Toys, tools, and technology shape people's experiences and their symbols. The children of Telstar are growing up in a learning environment which has been—and forever will be—conditioned by circling satellites, flying objects, countless cables, thousands of channels, and a box of lights and wires. The sources of electronic education are beyond the home or school and are structured neither by established curriculum nor by elected school board. As a special audience, children need their elders to regulate this technology for them until they are mature enough to manage it for themselves.

The protection of the young through law is not a new development in this democracy or its British antecedent. Child labor laws were instituted to protect the young who were being employed in the marketplace and exploited by adults. Similarly, compulsory education was established to insure the development of human intellectual resources. Government did not leave these options either to parents or private enterprise; it sensed that ultimately everybody's children are the concern of the society as a whole.

Precedent for regulation can be found in English law of 200 years ago when judges began creating special rules for situations involving children. In the feudal ages a "man's home was his castle." He could do whatever he wished to anyone who might trespass on his property. It was thought that property ownership accorded full and complete rights of possession.

By the middle of the 18th century, the Industrial Revolution had already begun to change values in England. Women began to work in the textile mills of Manchester. With fathers and mothers working in many families, increasing numbers of children were roaming the streets unattended.

We are taught by the basic case *Rylands* v. *Fletcher* that a child in England once wandered onto a vacant estate while walking his dog and his foot triggered a spring gun as it touched one of the attached wires along the ground. The judge ruled that the earlier notions of property law no longer pertained. It was unconscionable, said the judge, that an innocent, wandering child should be allowed to be harmed by an absentee property owner who employed such acts. If a person were to place spring guns on his property, he would be liable for a higher standard of care; that is, he would be held responsible for any harm caused by the spring gun. This is the concept of strict liability.

In tort law, if you are *negligent*, you are normally liable for the harm done. If you willfully assault or batter someone, you are liable for the harm done. If you keep explosives, strict liability applies because of their inherently dangerous nature. Any harm caused by them would thus normally make the owner liable.

Another concept of protection that had its origin in British common law is that of "attractive nuisance," which says that an owner or manager who creates something that is highly alluring but potentially harmful should be held to higher standards of responsibility than usual. A property owner who has swimming holes or who builds a swimming pool may not assume that children or others might not wander into it and subsequently be injured; he is therefore required to build a fence around it. Similarly, if you own oceanfront property (and cannot build a fence around the ocean), you are still responsible for people who might be harmed and are expected to put up lights or warnings: sharks, jellyfish, undertow, etc. Usually, under law, a person is liable only for acts (or omissions) only when he or she is negligent. But as manager of an "attractive nuisance," the pool owner is held to strict liability and is responsible for any harm done by the alluring and attractive nuisance.

Television also should be thought of as an alluring and attractive nuisance. Children are magically drawn to it and often suffer harm (or negative effects) because of this attraction. Although, technically, all the citizens own the airwaves on which television operates, the Federal Communications Commission (FCC) is the "manager" or trustee, appointed by Congress, to regulate the use of broadcast media. As manager of TV, as an attractive nuisance, the FCC should bear more responsibility for the potential harm done to children and could do this by insisting on higher standards and distinguished service by broadcasters and advertisers who use this public property. Can we believe that after luring the child to the set, the broadcaster has no responsibility for harm done there?

Habitual viewing has been called into question as a matter of public health, as it is known to affect the child's basic outlook, self-image, predisposition to violence, attitudes about sexuality, language development, nutrition, and eating habits. Somehow we have arrived at the thirtieth birthday of television to see that we have not harnessed the energies of the medium to serve the basic needs of children.

TO "SERVE THE PUBLIC INTEREST"

The national policy for the U.S. broadcasting system was set up in the Communications Act of 1934. This policy allows for private ownership of TV stations, with an administrative agency, the FCC, overseeing these private interests and regulating their operations. While all citizens own the airwaves, the FCC is named as trustee or manager.

Congress said that in exchange for the license to use the public's airwaves, the station owners must operate to "serve the public interest," and that while broadcasters may earn profits, they must subordinate their profitmaking to their obligation to serve the public interest. Every three years, station owners must reapply for their licenses, but the renewal application may be denied if it can be demonstrated that the station has not served the public interest. But what does it mean to serve the public interest?

What definitions we have came to us through the courts (not through regulatory agencies) in case-by-case examination of alleged abuses. For example, the broadcast reform movement was propelled by the landmark WLBT case in which the U.S. Court of Appeals revoked the license of that station in Jackson, Mississippi, on the grounds that WLBT neglected the public interest by consistently avoiding opportunities to televise images concerning Blacks. The case also established the right of consumer groups to have their views made part of official license-renewal proceedings and proved the effectiveness of the *petition to deny* as a tool for change.

When the license came up for renewal in the mid-sixties, the Office of Communication of the United Church of Christ, in New York, had joined with Black leaders in Jackson to file against WLBT. They documented on-the-air discrimination against Black people in a community whose potential viewing population was 45 percent Black. In 1969 the court ordered the FCC to deny renewal and award the broadcasting privilege to a more deserving applicant.

With the WLBT decision, the grassroots movement flowered. All around the country, broadcasters who had snubbed dissatisfied consumer groups began to entertain dialogues with them in preference to facing the onerous and costly petition to deny. This was the first time that a license-renewal application had been denied specifically for failure to serve *the public interest of children*.

EARLY DAYS

When television came to life in the late 1940's, its children's shows were characterized by puppets and whimsy, pie-throwing and silliness—in short, innocence. Among the earliest children's shows were *Kukla, Fran and Ollie; Howdy Doody; Ding Dong School; Mr. I Magination; Superman;* and *Hopalong Cassidy* (adapted from radio). About half of the children's shows in this era were presented without commercials. Then in the early fifties came *Rootie, Time for Beany, Zoo Parade, Super Circus, Pinky Lee, Big Top, Watch Mr. Wizard, Rin Tin Tin, Captain Video, Lucky Pup,* and *Juvenile Jury;* and, subsequently, *Lassie, Disneyland, The Shari Lewis Show,* and *Captain Kangaroo.*

The shows of the 1940's and early 1950's were intended to charm audiences and prompt the wealthier families to buy sets by demonstrating some of the good things that television can do. By the mid-1960's, when most of the households had one set, programs were aimed at the children on the theory that children controlled the dial and the family's viewing until bedtime.

Les Brown, of *The New York Times,* has pointed out that children helped to build the audience for stations and aided the growing enthusiasm for television, but they were not initially perceived as an advertising *market,* a situation that was bound to change as the proliferation of multiset households, the trend to participation advertising, and the discovery of a "pure" audience of children on Saturday mornings became business factors by the mid-1960's.

Hence, the youth market was born, and children's programming became a network profit center. Brown says:

> Citizens groups did not become aroused, however, until the networks began to deal excessively—in their competitive zeal—with monsters, grotesque superheros and gratuitous violence to win the attention of youngsters. Advertisers, by then, were making the most of the gullibility of children by pitching sugar-coated cereals

and candy-coated vitamins and expensive toys (some retailing for as much as $50) in shrewdly made commercials that often verged on outright deception.

Disgusted with this, the originators of *Sesame Street* aimed to produce a program for preschoolers that would teach children something useful while entertaining them. Other encouraging programs became available about the same time: *Mr. Rogers' Neighborhood, Zoom, Big Blue Marble*, the bilingual programs *Villa Alegre* and *Carrascolendas* on public television, and occasional positive entries by commercial TV, such as ABC's afterschool specials. The long-standing pillar of positive programming for kids is *Captain Kangaroo* (CBS), which debuted in 1955 and has been running ever since. *Captain* was, and is, the only daily program for children on the networks.

Unfortunately, these kinds of programs are only a tiny fraction of the total television that children watch. Heavy viewing patterns persist, and generally children watch more and more television each year no matter what the programs are. To some degree preschoolers are guided to the more appropriate programs for them, but for the most part children roam the time zones and content areas—unaccompanied by their parents.

As a parent who mediates and limits TV with children in our home, I feel that I am carrying out a parental responsibility. As a citizen it concerns me to know, however, that millions of children in our country are victims of inappropriate TV experience—through no fault of their own—because their parents are either not home, unaware of the dangers, or are uncaring, and because the TV they watch tends to be mediocre or worse. It is in the best interest of the society to offer some protection to the millions of children who watch more than 30 hours a week. New standards in programming and advertising are needed.

ACT IS BORN

Dismayed and angered by video violence and TV cereal

commercials, a dozen parents met one evening in 1968 in a home in Newtonville, Massachusetts, to plan a movement that they hoped would improve the TV viewing experience for all children. Television is here to stay, they reasoned, and therefore it should be improved. They formed Action for Children's Television (ACT). Peggy Charren, its president (then and now), says, "When I started ACT, my youngest daughter was seven and I was thinking about careers—but I thought I'd first take one year to fix up children's television, and then go back to work."

Today ACT is a national nonprofit consumer organization working to encourage diversity and quality in children's television. It initiates legal reform through petitions to the Federal regulatory agencies (FCC and FTC) and promotes public awareness of issues relating to children's television through public-education campaigns, publications, national conferences, and speaking engagements. ACT has over 15,000 members in the United States and the support of many major institutions concerned with children.

The group's success has disturbed the TV business and caused at least one vice-president to call ACT the enemy, while another executive has called it "an ally for me to go to my management and get a dollar commitment for better programming."

ACT has consistently pressed for *rules*, contending that an industry that invests hundreds of millions of dollars in advertising to children cannot be objective enough to regulate itself. According to ACT, the NAB Code has not produced enough "self-regulation" in TV, and the industry lacks suffi-cient commitment to do so. (The NAB, or National Association of Broadcasters, is the major trade association of the U.S. broadcast industry. It speaks for the industry on policy matters and creates codes for its voluntary membership. Transgressors of the Code's principles may be punished only by being denied the privilege of displaying the NAB seal.)

As a result of the pressure exerted by ACT, some important "voluntary" changes have been made, including:

- Reduction of Saturday morning children's advertising time by 40 percent (compared with the late sixties).
- Elimination of vitamin pill advertising on children's programs.
- More diversity in TV offerings for children.
- Elimination of "host" commercials on children's programs.

WAR DECLARED ON AD-BAN

ACT's most controversial move (still in progress) is its campaign to rid kids' programming of commercials altogether and establish minimum time standards for children's programming. ACT rocked the boat so vigorously throughout the 1970's that by the end of the decade the Federal Trade Commission had issued a staff report recommending:

- A ban on all television advertising directed to children under eight (on grounds that they are too young to understand the commercial intent of ads).
- A ban on television advertising to children between ages eight and twelve of the highly sugared foods most likely to promote dental decay (on grounds that they cannot evaluate the dental risks involved in eating highly sugared foods).
- Corrective advertising (nutritional disclosures) to balance commercials for other sugared foods (on grounds that children cannot make discriminating choices about diet and nutrition unless they are given more complete information than is presented in current ads).

In 1979 the FTC began public hearings on the proposals; hundreds of experts were called to testify. (A detailed chronology of ACT's reform efforts from 1968 to the present appears in Appendix C, p. 213.) The broadcasters, advertisers, and product manufacturers joined forces to fight the consumerists whom they now perceived as a threat to their profits. The broadcasters and advertisers raised a $30-million war chest to fight the consumers. In economic terms, it's a David and Goliath battle. While the industry inhabits glass skyscrapers in New York, ACT works with a limited budget out of the second story of a turn-of-the-century house. While ACT has only one in-house attorney working on this complicated legal question, the adversary has about 50 lawyers assigned to the matter and has also hired two of New York's largest public relations firms to help "stop Peggy." Troops mobilized, war chest raised, the broadcasting industry's strategy is to move into the halls of Congress and the regulatory agencies to lobby against new standards or regulation for children's TV. Or, to put it in the words of the vice-president and general counsel of the National Association of Broadcasters (NAB), John Summers, to ". . . go to the commissioners and lobby the hell out of them on children's TV."

Children have the same right as adults to be protected against deceptive commercial speech. Broadcasters routinely protect adults from deceptive commercials, and ACT is looking for similar protection for children. It is the child advocates' further position that the young have an even more basic need for protection—in order to grow. They should be protected from TV advertising because they do not—cannot—understand its messages or intent, nor do they have the judgment to make decisions about what is good for them to want, to nag for, and to consume. In this sense, all advertising aimed at children is inherently unfair. This, however, does not prevent them from becoming incessant beggars in the aisles of the supermarkets of America.

Inevitably, the industry will say: Yes, we too believe in protecting the young, but is the proposed FTC ban the way to do it? Let parents do it. However, in terms of psychodynamics, a parent is inevitably frustrated by his or her inability to screen TV commercials before broadcast. Probably no parent has time or inclination to sit and watch every TV show that children view. Even if this were the case, no parent, even if he or she had the talent to be more persuasive than the TV, could interrupt the ads to offer alternative explanations. Further, no matter how willing and able a parent is to spend time watching with a child, he or she is handicapped by not knowing at which instant something objectionable will appear. So, despite well-meaning attempts, a parent would never be able to anticipate and dilute or erase commercial messages that later seem unsatisfactory for the young.

Once the commercial message has registered and the begging for products has begun, the parent has the option to say "no"—but saying "no" for TV products seriously increases the negative function of the parent. Parents have to say "no" to many things—and to increase this load by having to say "no" to hundreds of commercials each week is a ridiculous burden in light of the tremendous responsibilities that parents face.

Some pose the question of the First Amendment. Designed to protect freedom of speech, it does not permit *anyone* to say *anything* to anybody *anytime*. You may not yell "Fire!" in a crowded theater, and you may not advertise cigarettes on television, because they were declared hazardous to health and ruled off the air. Junk foods are equally as hazardous to children's health as cigarettes are to that of adults, according to experts. Clearly, the First Amendment prevents anyone from putting a heavy regulatory hand on programming, but nonprogram, deceptive commercial speech is another matter.

The child advocates' position holds that consuming TV commercials serves only to add to the confusion, exploitation, and misinformation that children must cope with, a position that puts respect for the basic needs of the child ahead of the commercial needs of the advertisers.

ACTING ON VIOLENCE

Outraged at the levels of TV violence, ACT started out in 1968 with the conviction that children should be treated as a special audience. Careful study showed ACT's founders that *advertising* is the underlying cause for much violent children's programming because violent action draws the largest share of the two-to-eleven-year-old audience to the screen for the commercial message. ACT then developed a campaign to encourage *diversity* in children's programming as one means of cutting down on violence. In a system based on scarcity of channels, this approach can work. By reason, as the level of diversity increases, the percentage of violent programs must decrease.

ACT began its continuing campaign for diversity and quality in children's programming in the spring of 1970 when its leaders met with six of the seven Federal Communications Commissioners to talk about the need for overall regulation of children's TV and to present a petition to eliminate ads from children's programs. Peggy Charren recalls, "Never before had a citizen called up and asked to meet with the FCC." (See the ACT Chronology, Appendix C, p. 213).

In addition to asking the Commission to make rules banning advertising on children's programming, ACT asked it to require certain amounts of children's programming throughout the week as well as on weekends. After four years of consideration the FCC refused to make rules to protect children but instead (in 1974) turned the requests into a set of guidelines titled "Children's Television Policy Statement." The guidelines, which cannot be enforced, say that all TV stations must provide a reasonable amount of children's programming and that much of it should be informational and educational.

Largely through the pressure created by ACT, the networks shifted to more wholesome shows and cut back commercial announcements in weekend children's shows from 16 minutes per hour to 9½. But little else changed. In 1978, at ACT's urging, the commission embarked on a "second inquiry" to see if anything had changed. Soon the commission is to announce whether or not it will recommend regulation as a response to inaction.

Some other citizens groups have made minor changes at the local level. A group in Los Angeles, the National Association for Better Broadcasting (NABB), filed a petition to deny the license of station KTTV on grounds that its highly violent programming did not properly serve the public interest of children. In negotiations, KTTV agreed to remove from the air 42 series (including *Batman*, *Superman*, *Spiderman*, *The Wild, Wild West*, and others) and to post warnings to parents for a list of 81 other shows if they were aired before 8:30 P.M. However, the FCC overturned the agreement, saying that "deals" between citizen groups and stations could not be made because they had the effect of program censorship. In Lansing, Michigan, the Citizens for Better Broadcasting persuaded WJIM-TV, the CBS affiliate, to switch reruns of the rough program *The Wild, Wild West* from its afterschool time slot to a later hour, thus reducing the numbers of children in the audience.

The PTA held regional hearings on televised violence in the late 1970's. Westinghouse Broadcasting President Donald McGannon decried the lack of alternatives in network programming and asserted, "False and insensitive elements are being injected into programs to build audience."

When Dr. Michael Rothenberg described the "national scandal" over TV violence in the *Journal of the American Medical Association (JAMA)*, the organization set up a collective cry of protest against television programming from the profession. Since then, the AMA has held in-service conferences and funded research and social action. One medic recommended:

> The AMA, if it is really ready to fight this environmental disease, should appoint a panel that will identify the programs most notorious for their routine and persistent portrayal of violence. Once those programs have been so identified, let the list be posted in doctors' offices. The application of the boycott is then straightforward: those who believe that violence on TV must be contained will simply pledge themselves not to purchase products promoted in association with the offending programs. Our dogs, after all, can survive even if they have to do without any canine gourmet dish that happens to underwrite a weekly gangland-police shoot-out, and our kitchens will function without electronic devices promoted between gory executions and garrottings.

Action against violence was accelerated when the National Citizens' Committee for Broadcasting (NCCB) in Washington began publishing the "ten most violent" programs and their sponsors, with funding from the AMA. The NCCB, led by Nicholas Johnson, designed a study ranking TV series in terms of violent content. The rankings, based on a six-week computer survey of prime-time shows, also named sponsors of the most violent shows. The study employed the violence definition and coding system developed by Dr. George Gerbner, dean of the Annenberg School of Communications, and his colleague, Dr. Larry Gross. The tabulation of aggressive acts results in a "violence index" that offers a means of making comparisons on a program-to-program or season-to-season basis. Publishing the list of violent shows caused some embarrassed advertisers—considering it good business to try to avoid boycotts by affluent consumers who may want to protest TV violence—to find new places to sell their wares.

Some television executives termed the NCCB strategy an unfairly coercive one, although Johnson thought of the published violence lists as a "consumer report" on TV content, a way of blowing the whistle or pointing a finger at "who's manufacturing what" in the way of TV images.

More and more people are recommending a "medical model" that would put the responsibility on the introducer of a new product to demonstrate why it should enter the mainstream of life. For example, in order to market a new drug, its creator must demonstrate to the Federal Drug Administration (FDA) its safety and usefulness to the public before approval is awarded. This practice offers protection for consumers. In other words, the regulatory agency says to creators, "You tell us why this product is good for the people,"—rather than requiring the public to demonstrate, after unhealthful experiences, why it is "bad" for people.

Applied to the TV business, this suggests that the networks should have to produce evidence to show why violence is good for children rather than burdening public-interest groups or other child advocates to show why it is not good for children to be consuming this product.

The real question about violence on TV is why it should be a part of children's programming at all. As Dr. Anna Freud pointed out, the need of the child is to spend his energies struggling with his own innate aggression and not with everything that comes to him from outside.

Brenda Grayson, a twenty-eight-year-old Black TV producer, who grew up in Harlem, says:

> I wouldn't have any violence in children's television. There is no need to present more negative solutions to kids who already have too many in real life. People in the inner-city have lots of positive uses for aggression. They can harness that energy to get themselves off welfare or overcome educational deficiencies. TV violence doesn't serve any basic need of the child.

Says Les Brown, TV correspondent to *The New York Times:*

> Tell me why a big-city station in the midwest can deal excessively in violent programming—knowing that one-third of its audience is children—and still be thought to be serving the public interest. The fact that people watch does not mean that you are serving the public interest; distinguished service, which is the duty, may be quite another thing. The FCC rubber-stamps station licenses; it has never taken away a license for failure to serve the public interest.

Northrop Frye, commissioner on the Canadian Radio and Television Commission (CRTC), Canada's regulatory agency, has another perception of TV violence:

> Apart from outright crime, which is now a business like any other, there are many activities which are still legal but are morally wrong. When a broadcaster and a sponsor conspire to produce a socially irresponsible program, that is in itself a violent situation, and has to be recognized as such.

To be socially responsible to children, television must somehow play to their *basic needs.* No one has demonstrated that exposure to TV violence serves any basic need of any child anywhere. What is most outrageous is that we are conditioning people to the notion of "violence as entertainment." A humanist approach would require broadcasters who want to use violence as TV entertainment to first demonstrate why this is good for the physical, emotional, intellectual, or spiritual health of the society.

REMAINING QUESTIONS

The political storm at the regulatory agencies (now spreading to Congress) has to do not only with children's TV but with the entire concept of regulation. At the same moment that some citizens are pushing for stiffer regulations, others are vigorously advocating abolishing the regulatory structure altogether! The Department of Justice has suggested that even the (voluntary) NAB Code, which suggests limiting advertising minutes to nine and a half minutes per hour, may be a "restraint of trade." As discussed in the section on proposed FTC advertising regulation, enormous lobbies with budgets of millions of dollars have been set up to see that profits are protected by whatever public policy the commissions may create. Peggy Charren, president of Action for Children's Television, speaks about consumer protection in general:

> We feel that the system set up by Government to protect the public from manipulation by monied interests should work. What affects us more than the money being spent against ACT and children on this issue [ad regulation] is the attempt to change the balance of power so that the public interest is undermined. The fact that industry lobbies can successfully muzzle regulatory agencies is a frightening precedent that could affect many aspects of life in this country.

In light of the opposition to government regulation, some important questions must be asked. When the TV station becomes a data bank, who will regulate the use of that information? Will the purveyors of pornography enter the home or will extremists gain access to audiences through proliferating cable channels? Who will control the communications satellites? Who is responsible when violence (made in America) is syndicated to many countries of the world?

When we talk about the *content* of TV programs rather than commercials, thoughts of government regulation must be modified. When we think about curtailing TV violence or building up the quality in TV programming, we must turn to a number of other methods.

HOW TO WORK FOR DIVERSITY IN PROGRAMMING

One way to promote quality programming is to aim for greater diversity in the fare that is beamed into our homes. Television now seeks the largest possible audience for each program in order to present more products to potential buyers. As a result, TV finds the lowest common denominator in mass taste. Minorities numbering in the millions now find their tastes and needs ignored. Greater diversity of programming would offer people a choice—for better or worse, but new program opportunities would inevitably meet more needs. Nelson Price, a creator of the "Television Awareness Training" process, once pointed out that making a choice among three network prime-time programs is something like going out to dinner and "choosing" between McDonalds, Burger King, and Burger Chef.

Fortunately, in this democracy, there are ways for citizens to promote diversity. Some actions may be taken by individuals but others require groups or highly organized lobbies—because television itself is a big business which is influenced by vested-interest lobbies.

Express your opinion. One effective way to do this is to write letters to local stations, networks and sponsors, FCC, FTC, and congressional representatives. These letters will be read, counted, analyzed, and answered. They may be tallied in terms of both the issue and the program in question. Letters that illustrate a point of view may be circulated among staff. If you think that the FCC should enforce the policy (or turn it into rules) which states that every station must provide a minimal amount of quality programming for children, you must write the FCC to say so!

"There's no reason under the First Amendment why you can't express your views to sponsors," said Dr. Everett C. Parker, director of the Office of Communications of the United Church of Christ. "People have a right to speak out. That's what the First Amendment is all about. But this is not just a First Amendment question . . . it is a matter of protecting family life and children, covered by other amendments to the Constitution."

To prepare effective letters to broadcasters and sponsors, you should:

- Clarify your values. Ask yourself, how do I feel about solving problems with force? Or about the use of gratuitous violence as entertainment? Which aspects of sexuality should be sanctioned by television, and how? Should children be protected from certain TV images?
- Make your point briefly. Write in direct, short sentences.
- Speak about a specific TV situation. State what you saw or heard, and at what time. Be thoughtful and factual. Bombastic language tends to discount the criticism. For example, the letter cited previously: "Last night (date) at 8:15 my children and I saw an NBC promotional ad for *Police Woman*, which is a program aired at 10 P.M. This ad showed a man beating up his wife while a young child looked on from the crib. Angry shouting and screaming accompanied the beating."
- State your response to the TV image. "If this is not a program produced for children, neither should it be advertised to children. This ad incites fears, presents violence, and acts as a lure to make them want to stay up late and see what is not good for them. As such, it does not serve the public interest."
- Write as an individual rather than someone on orders from a group. However, if you have an organizational affiliation, be sure to mention it.
- Type your letter if possible.
- Send carbon copies to interested parties such as advertisers, reform groups, regulatory agencies, and representatives in Congress.

• Address your letter to the chief of the organization: presidents of networks or sponsoring companies, chairpersons of the FCC or FTC, and general managers of your local television stations.
• Sign your name to the original and carbon copy.[1]

The powers of letter writing have been demonstrated. In 1970, when ACT filed a petition with the FCC asking it to ban commercials on children's television programs and to require all stations to provide at least 14 hours a week of children's programming suited to the needs of various-aged children, the commission was deluged with 100,000 letters from all parts of the country supporting the petition. The commission subsequently issued guidelines (1974) for children's TV based on ACT's original petition.

Similarly, citizen response to the published violence ratings of the National Citizens' Committee for Broadcasting caused some sponsors to withdraw ads from violent shows. Letters to sponsors have helped to point out public opinion about violence.

In addition to acting as an individual, you may join groups or coalitions which also voice opinions. (See National Research and Reform Groups, Appendix E, p. 222.) For example:

• The National Citizens' Committee for Broadcasting (NCCB) in Washington, D.C., headed by Nicholas Johnson and Ralph Nader, which coordinates citizens' group efforts, represents reformist views at the FCC and congressional hearings, promotes a citizens' lobby, and publishes a journal, *access*.
• Action for Children's Television (ACT), which works to promote quality children's programming without commercialism and publishes a magazine, *re:act*.
• Office of Communication of the United Church of Christ, in New York, led by Everett Parker, devoted to aiding minorities in broadcasting and studying the policy issues involved in the Communications Act.
• National Association for Better Broadcasting (NABB), in Los Angeles, which publishes a critique of programs on

the air and has successfully pressured stations to remove violent children's programs.
- Minority rights organizations such as the National Organization for Women (NOW), the Mexican-American Council, the Gay Media Task Force, and the National Black Media Coalition.

Develop alternate sources of funding for programs via group action. For the most part children's television has been funded by advertisers' dollars (and the necessity of mass audience), which has prompted the production of cheap and easy cartoons which will attract a large audience, without regard to values, portrayals, or other literary qualities.

Other sources of funding for quality children's programming could come from corporate underwriting, network productions for children, and various forms of pay television. International Telephone & Telegraph (ITT) spent over $10 million on *Big Blue Marble,* underwriting the cost of research and development, production, syndication, support material for schools, and public relations. Over 100 half-hours have been created and the program is still in production. ITT provides the show *free* to stations which will run it without commercials. At the time *Big Blue Marble* began in 1973, ITT was looking for a public-service project. People were beginning to become aware of children's needs in TV, there was little for the preteen audience, and nothing on the air showed children around the world.

Another method of funding that has been proposed would require networks to assume the costs of some children's production as a way of serving the public interest. Some portion of the tremendous profits accrued in advertising to adults could be recycled in children's programs. (In 1950 about half of the children's programming on the air appeared without ads and was paid for by the networks.)[2] Still other funding possibilities are suggested by the fact that cable TV, offering scores of channels to each receiver, will be available in 30 percent of U.S. homes by 1988. The proliferation of cable will increase the "pay-TV" possibility in which certain programs that you pay for can be received into your home.

Recognize and reward quality programs via group or coalition action. Broadcasters should be encouraged to continue those efforts they have made to provide good programming for children. ACT expresses positive opinions by means of annual "Achievement in Children's Television" awards for both commercial and public broadcasters' programs or series. ACT has commended corporations for funding outstanding programming and recently recognized a local station that refused to air commercials for highly sugared products during its daily children's shows. A few of the programs that have received ACT awards are *ABC Afterschool and Weekend Specials, Rebop, Once Upon a Classic, Captain Kangaroo, In the News, Sesame Street, Mr. Rogers' Neighborhood, Big Blue Marble, The CBS Children's Film Festival,* and *Fat Albert and the Cosby Kids.*

Develop a consortium of leaders and creators. This group could frame goals and contents for a channel devoted to children's programming. Every community will soon have a study committee on cable TV. Join it. As cable TV will provide new outlets, there will no longer be a scarcity of channels. One expert explains: "While present cable systems carry up to 36 channels, when the copper cables are replaced with thin glass fibers (fiberoptics) which use laser beams as light sources, homes could receive as many as 1,000 channels. It is not too early to ask questions that we weren't asking of the present system."

Establish an international children's programming exchange or clearinghouse via group action. This organization could match existing programming with outlets and audiences. Wider program sharing could occur through information sharing. All of the existing programs from any country in the world could be registered for possible syndication. Such an institute could offer options to the programmer of a small station in a developing country which is just establishing TV for the first time or to the cable station with a children's channel. Might it not be better for a child in Jamaica to grow up with programs produced in Mexico or Singapore than on a diet of white role models? Surely there is more locally produced programming available than is indicated in the catalogs of American syndicators?

Such a clearinghouse could also serve as a rallying point for the thousands of writers, artists, and creators who need to know each other and to find potential audiences. Such an information exchange would help to promote quality children's programming by making available diverse alternatives for the creator who, in the past, has had to pander to the requirements of large, commercial U.S. systems.

IS THERE HOPE FOR CHILDREN'S TV?

I believe that the medium which can teach us to be fearful or cynical can also be used to help children learn how to trust, to care, to comprehend, to feel good about themselves. So does the woman who wrote to Fred Rogers of *Mr. Rogers' Neighborhood:*

> I have a nine-year-old girl with brain dysfunction. She has so many social failures at home, at school and at play that she has a very bad self-image. She has always loved your program, and one day I listened while she was watching. You were singing and I listened to the words—"I like you just the way you are." And tears came to my eyes as I realized that you were doing for this disagreeable little child what none of us here were able to do. God bless you for opening my eyes.

Other positive feelings come up when Captain Kangaroo reminds children to "share what you have to share" or *Sesame Street* shows kids of all colors having a good time together.

These "good" programs exist, however, in an ocean of garbage (made for children) which virtually covers the world: *Popeye, Batman, Birdman, Spiderman, Gigantor, Dastardly and Muttley, Josie and the Pussycats, The Banana Splits, I Dream of Jeannie, The Flintstones,* etc.

The new box made of lights, wires, and winking dots has documented the great events of our times, has brought the arts to everybody, and has entertained us. It can teach many things and can serve us in the ways that we want it to serve us. Television isn't hopeless because we are not helpless.

But we are going to have to harness the energy of television, or it will harness us. We must pursue all questions vigorously: What might it mean to serve the public interest of children? What does diversity in programming mean? What is quality children's programming? What basic needs of children can TV address?

Even with incomplete information, a person can figure out how his or her children can live sensibly with this new medium. We can study television, we can think about the quality we want for our lives, and we can make judgments and decisions. We can come to terms with television by broadening real-life relationships, by limiting time spent mindlessly with TV, and by creating diverse and culturally enriching programming. Whatever the world may turn out to be like a generation from now, one thing is sure: In order to live with a sense of meaning, dignity, and worth, the grandchildren of Telstar will have to be able to do much more than passively watch a box in the corner.

APPENDIX A
READ-ALOUD BOOKS

Note: A prerequisite for reading is an amicable relationship with books. Adults can build the child's relationship with print by reading aloud each day. The custom should begin in the preschool years and continue as long as possible—especially throughout the elementary school years. To assemble this list of recommendations, I talked with parents, teachers, librarians—and Captain Kangaroo, who has read books to children on TV for 25 years—asking them to suggest titles that are popular with most children including boys and girls, children of diverse ethnic backgrounds, and children at various levels of mental maturity. Of course, there are many wonderful books that are not included here; you will discover them as you explore children's literature by reading aloud to young people. Experience has shown that when the adult reader is genuinely delighted by the book that he or she is reading out loud, that joy is communicated to the child who is listening. Please choose accordingly.

Preschool and Kindergarten

Amos and Boris, William Steig, Farrar, Straus and Giroux, 1971.
Angus and the Ducks, Marjorie Flack, Doubleday, 1943.
Ask Mr. Bear, Marjorie Flack, Macmillan, 1932.
The Birthday, Hans Fischer, Harcourt, 1954.
Blueberries for Sal, Robert McCloskey, Viking, 1948.
Book of Nursery and Mother Goose Rhymes, (comp. and ill.) Marguerite de Anegeli, Doubleday, 1954.
The Cat in the Hat, Dr. Seuss, Random House, 1957.
A Child's Garden of Verses, Robert Louis Stevenson, Grosset & Dunlap, 1957.
Country Bunny and the Little Gold Shoes, DuBose Heyward, Houghton, 1939.
Curious George, H. A. Rey, Houghton, 1941.
Dandelion, Don Freeman, Viking, 1964.
The Day Daddy Stayed Home, Ethel Kessler, Doubleday, 1959.

"The Elephant's Child," from *Just So Stories*, Rudyard Kipling, Doubleday (many ed.).

The 500 Hats of Bartholomew Cubbins, Dr. Seuss, Vanguard, 1938.

Gilberto and the Wind, Marie Hall Ets, Viking, 1963.

Golden Books (the series), Golden Press.

Goodnight Moon, Margaret Wise Brown, Harper, 1947.

The Growing Story, Ruth Krauss, Harper, 1947.

Harry, The Dirty Dog, Gene Zion, Harper, 1956.

Inch by Inch, Leo Lionni, Obolensky, 1960.

Lentil, Robert McCloskey, Viking, 1940.

Leo the Late Bloomer, Robert Kraus, paperback only, 1973.

Little Bear (series), Else Minarik, Harper, 1957.

Little Blue and Little Yellow, Leo Lionni, Obolensky, 1959.

Lyle, Lyle Crocodile, Bernard Waber, Houghton, 1965.

Madeline's Rescue, Ludwig Bemelmans, Viking, 1954.

Make Way for Ducklings, Robert McCloskey, Viking, 1941.

Miffy (series), Dick Bruna, Methuen Inc.

Mike Mulligan and His Steam Shovel, Virginia L. Burton, Houghton, 1939.

Millions of Cats, Wanda Gag, Coward, 1928.

Mommies at Work, Eve Merriam, Knopf, 1961.

My Mother Is the Most Beautiful Woman in the World, Rebecca Reyher, Howell Suskin, 1945.

The Night Before Christmas, Clement Moore (many ed.).

Play With Me, Marie Hall Ets, Viking, 1955.

Put Me in the Zoo, Robert Lopshire, Random House, 1960.

Real Book of Mother Goose, Blanche F. Wright, McNally, 1916.

The Red Balloon, Albert Lamorisse, Doubleday, 1956.

The Runaway Bunny, Margaret Wise Brown, Harper, 1942.

The Snowy Day, Ezra Jack Keats, Viking, 1962.

Stone Soup, Marcia Brown, Scribner, 1947.

A Story—A Story, Gail E. Haley, Atheneum, 1970.

The Story of Babar, Jean De Brunhoff, Random House, 1933.

Sylvester and the Magic Pebble, William Steig, Simon & Schuster, 1969.

The Tale of Peter Rabbit, Beatrix Potter, Warne, 1903.

Tikki Tikki Tembo, Arlene Mosel, Holt, 1968.

Tirra Lirra, Laura E. Richards, Little, 1955 ed.

Wait for William, Marjorie Flack, Houghton, 1935.

What Do People Do All Day, Richard Scarry, Random House, 1968.

When We Were Very Young, A. A. Milne, Dutton, 1924.

Where the Wild Things Are, Maurice Sendak, Harper, 1963.
William's Doll, Charlotte Zolotow, Harper, 1972.
Winnie the Pooh, A. A. Milne, Dutton, 1926.

First and Second Grades

(Note: Parents and teachers should continue to select books from the Kindergarten list.)

The Amiable Giant, Louis Slobodkin, Macmillan, 1955.
Baby Sister for Frances, Russell Hoban, Harper, 1964.
The Bears on Hemlock Mountain, Alice Dalgleish, Scribner, 1952.
Bedtime for Frances, Russell Hoban, Harper, 1960.
Bread and Jam for Frances, Russell Hoban, Harper, 1964.
Chicken Soup with Rice, Maurice Sendak, Harper, 1962.
Curious George Rides a Bike, H. A. Rey, Houghton, 1952.
The Duchess Bakes a Cake, Virginia Kahl, Scribner, 1955.
Five Chinese Brothers, Claire H. Bishop, Coward, 1938.
The Hole in the Tree, Jean George, Dutton, 1957.
"How the Camel Got His Hump," from the *Just So Stories*, Rudyard Kipling, Doubleday (many ed.).
The Hundred Penny Box, Sharon Bell Mathis, Viking, 1975.
Katy and the Big Snow, Virginia L. Burton, Houghton, 1943.
Little Fur Family, Margaret Wise Brown, Harper, 1968.
The Little House, Virginia L. Burton, Houghton, 1942.
The Little House in the Big Woods, Laura Ingalls Wilder, Harper, 1953.
The Little House on the Prairie, Laura Ingalls Wilder, Harper, 1953 ed.
Little Toot, Hardie Gramatky, Putnam, 1939.
Millions of Cats, Wanda Gag, Coward-McCann, 1928.
Mr. Popper's Penguins, Richard Atwater, Little, 1938.
Nine Days to Christmas, Marie H. Ets, Viking, 1959.
Now We Are Six, A. A. Milne, Dutton, 1961 ed.
Ola, Ingri and Edgar P. d'Aulaire, Doubleday, 1932.
One Morning in Maine, Robert McCloskey, Viking, 1952.
Pop Corn and Ma Goodness, Edna Mitchell Preston, Viking, 1969.
The Story of Babar the Little Elephant, Jean de Brunhoff, Random House, 1960.
The Story of Ping, Marjorie Flack, Viking, 1933.
The Tale of Benjamin Bunny, Beatrix Potter, Warne, 1904.
Time for Poetry, May H. Arbuthnot, ed., Scott Foresman, 1952.
Time of Wonder, Robert McCloskey, Viking, 1957.

Third and Fourth Grades

Alice in Wonderland, Lewis Carroll, World, 1946.

All Around the Town, Phyllis McGinley, Lippincott, 1948.

Amos Fortune Free Man, Elizabeth Yates, Dutton, 1950.

Andy and the Lion, James Daugherty, Viking, 1938.

Ben and Me, Robert Lawson, Little, 1939.

Boy of the Pyramids, Ruth F. Jones, Random House, 1952.

Chanticleer and the Fox, Barbara Cooney, Crowell, 1959.

Charlie and the Chocolate Factory, Roald Dahl, Knopf, 1964.

Charlotte's Web, E. B. White, Harper, 1952.

The Children of Noisy Village, Astrid Lindgren, Viking, 1962.

The Courage of Sarah Noble, Alice Dalgliesh, Scribner, 1954.

Crow Boy, Yaskimo Taro, Viking, 1955.

The Egg Tree, Katherine Milhous, Scribner, 1950.

The Enormous Egg, Oliver Butterworth, Little, 1956.

The Fables of Aesop, Ruth Spriggs, ed., Rand McNally, 1975.

Farmer Boy, Laura Ingalls Wilder, Harper, 1953.

The Fools of Chelm and Their History, Isaac Bashevis Singer, Farrar, Straus & Giroux, 1975.

Hailstones and Halibut Bones, Mary O'Neill (ill. Leonard Weisgard), Doubleday, 1961.

Henry Huggins, Beverly Cleary, Morrow, 1950.

Horton Hatches the Egg, Dr. Seuss, Random House, 1940.

James and the Giant Peach, Roald Dahl, Knopf, 1961.

The Little Island, Margaret W. Brown, Doubleday, 1946.

The Otter's Tale, Gavin Maxwell, Dutton, 1962.

Paddle-to-the-Sea, Holling C. Holling, Houghton, 1941.

Pippi Longstocking, Astrid Lindgren, Viking, 1950.

Rabbit Hill, Robert Lawson, Viking, 1944.

The Story of Dr. Dolittle, Hugh Lofting, Lippincott, 1920.

The Tailor of Gloucester, Beatrix Potter, Warne, 1903.

Tales of a Fourth Grade Nothing, Judy Blume, Dutton, 1972.

The Trumpet of the Swan, E. B. White, Harper, 1970.

Twenty and Ten, Claire H. Bishop, Viking, 1952.

When Clay Sings, Byrd Baylor, Scribner, 1972.

The Wind in the Willows, Kenneth Grahame, Heritage ed., 1944.

Zlateh the Goat, Isaac Bashevis Singer, Harper, 1966.

Fifth and Sixth Grades

Abraham Lincoln Grows Up, Carl Sandburg, Harcourt, 1928.
The Adventures of Tom Sawyer, Mark Twain (many ed.).
The Ark, Margot Benary-Isbert, Harcourt, 1953.
Banner in the Sky, James Ullman, Lippincott, 1954.
The Borrowers, Mary Norton, Harcourt, 1953.
Call It Courage, Armstrong Sperry, Macmillan, 1941.
Daniel Boone, James Daugherty, Viking, 1939.
From the Mixed-up Files of Mrs. Basil E. Frankweiler, E. L.
    Konigsburg, Atheneum, 1967.
The Heroes, Charles Kingsley, Macmillan, 1954 ed.
The Hobbit, J. R. R. Tolkien, Houghton, 1938.
Homer Price, Robert McCloskey, Viking, 1943.
The House of Sixty Fathers, Meindert De Jong, Harper, 1956.
Huckleberry Finn, Mark Twain (many ed.).
Imagination's Other Place, Helen Plotz, ed., Crowell, 1955.
Johnny Tremain, Esther Forbes, Houghton, 1943.
The Lion, Witch and the Wardrobe, C. S. Lewis, Collier (A Division of
    Macmillan), 1978 (first ed., 1970).
The Long Winter, Laura Ingalls Wilder, Harper, 1953 ed.
Mary Poppins, P. L. Travers, Harcourt, 1934.
My Side of the Mountain, Jean George, Dutton, 1960.
Onion John, Joseph Krumgold, Crowell, 1959.
Owls in the Family, Frank Mowat, Little, 1962.
The Railway Children, E. Nesbit, Ernest Benn Limited, London, 1957.
Some Merry Adventures of Robin Hood, Howard Pyle, Scribner, 1954.
Sounder, William H. Armstrong, Harper, 1969.
The Thirteen Clocks, James Thurber, Simon & Schuster, 1950.
Treasure Island, R. L. Stevenson, World, 1946.
Twenty-one Balloons, William Pene DuBois, Viking, 1947.
A Wrinkle in Time, Madeleine L'Engle, Farrar, Straus & Giroux, 1962.

APPENDIX B
SUGGESTED
EQUIPMENT
AND
MATERIALS

The following lists are taken from *The Integrated Day in the Primary School* by Mary Brown & Norman Precious.

Furnishing

Working surfaces

Tables should be of the type which are easy to move and, if possible, stackable and with formica tops. Some tables with large working surfaces, perhaps of the trestle type, are useful.

A few table tops which are hinged to the wall and can be put up or down make useful work and display areas.

Tables for display.

Attractive occasional tables for book corners, etc.

Benches with storage shelves underneath.

Raised platforms about 5 feet by 3 feet 6 inches and about 1 foot from the floor, again with an easily cleaned surface.

Various sizes of boxes or platform units for children to assemble their own raised areas.

Seating accommodation

Comfortable easy chairs, wooden chairs, cane chairs, benches, cushions, rugs, carpets.

Working areas

An area which can be completely blacked out, possibly by using a screen and material.

Booths where children can work quietly and undisturbed.

Book corner fitments, standing units, or book trolleys so that books may be displayed to show their front covers.

Three-sided screens which can be assembled for various uses and can be adjusted in height by fitting removable legs. These screens can be used for houses, shops, clinics, etc.

Storage and display

Pine board areas on walls at the right height for children to use, and if possible some of these areas should be covered or boarded so that children can work there and the pictures stay. This eliminates the selection of work for display. Easels hinged to the wall serve the same purpose.

Open lockers or locker units without doors and preferably with an individual small drawer for each child.

Fixed wall blackboard or double-sided easel-type board for children's use.

Some provision for storing dressing-up clothes, bricks, junk materials, etc., such as boxes, wire baskets, low cupboards, or office bean stalks.

Vases for flowers.

Large Equipment

Aquarium
Book shelves
Cages for pets, birds, and insects
Camera
Clock
Containers for water: transparent polythene on tubular legs, tin bath, rubber dinghy
Duplicating machine which children can use
Earphones
Electric cooker available for children's use
Kiln
Loom
Movie camera
Paper guillotines
Piano

Printing press
Projector and films, 8mm. and 16mm.
Racks
Reading laboratories
Reading master
Record player
Sewing machine
Slide projector
Tape recorders
Tray to hold wet sand, preferably on castors
Tray to hold dry sand, preferably on castors
Trolleys
Typewriter for children's use
Various types of teaching machines and calculators

Wardrobe for dressing-up
 clothes
Wireless
Woodwork bench

Adventure Playground Material

Area of grass and trees
Area for digging
Auto tires
Barrels
Bicycle wheels
Big boxes
Felled trees
Growing trees
Ladders
Old car with its gas tank filled
 with sand
Orange boxes
Pramwheels
Seesaw
Sewage pipes
Slide
Tree trunks
Water supply

Equipment for Physical Activity

Balancing bar
Balls of all sizes
Bats
Bean bags
Boxes
Canes
Hoops
Jumping stands
Ladder
Mats, large and small
Plank
Poles
Quoits

Racquets
Ropes
Rope ladder
Shuttlecocks
Skittles
Storming board
Trapeze
Trestles
Vaulting horse

Domestic-Corner Equipment

Baby carriage
Bandages
Blanket
Bowl
Camp bed
Chairs
Clothes horse
Cupboard
Dolls, wooden, rubber, and
 plastic
Dolls' clothes, washable
Domestic equipment for
 sweeping, polishing, dusting,
 scrubbing, washing, ironing,
 and cooking
Kettle
Knives and forks, plastic
Table
Tea set, ordinary size, plastic
Teddy bear
Telephone
Towels

Suggestions for Dressing-up Clothes

Aprons
Crowns
Doctor's coat
Fans

Glasses
Gloves
Hand mirror
Jewelry
Lengths of material for drapes
   and trains
Long mirror
Nurse's uniform
Policeman's uniform
Sailor's uniform
Shawls
Skirts
Stethoscope
Wings

Cookery Utensils

Basins
Cake tins
Clock
Cook's measure
Egg whisk
Jelly mold
Measuring jugs
Measuring spoons
Oven glove
Palette knife
Patty tins
Pie dishes
Recipes
Saucepans
Scales
Tea towel
Wooden spoon

Music

Bells
Castanets
Chime bars
Cymbals

Glockenspiel
Homemade instruments
Indian bells
Instruments from olden days
Instruments from other countries
Musical box
Orchestra instruments
Recorders
Records, classical and jazz
Tambourines
Tambours
Triangles
Tubular bells
Tuning forks
Xylophone
Zither

Puppets

Glove puppets
Marionettes
Ready-made puppets for the
   children to use, and materials
   to make their own
Puppet theaters: shadow, glove,
   marionette
Strong source of light

Woodwork

Balsa wood
Bamboo pieces
Bradawl
Brushes
Corrugated brads
Cotton reels
Cuphooks
Dowelling
Drill
Eyelets
Files

Fretsaw
Glue
Hammers
Hessian pockets, fixed to a
  batten (to hold tools)
Hinges
Nails of all sizes
Offcuts of wood and peg board,
  all shapes and sizes
Paint and brushes
Panel pins
Pincers
Plane, simple type
Pliers
Ratchet brace
Sandpaper
Saws
Screwdriver
Screws of all sizes
Tenon saw
Twist drills
Varnish
Vice
Wheels

Gardening Equipment

Cloches
Cold frames
Dibbler
Forks
Hoe
Lightweight roller
Line
Rake
Spades
Trowels
Watering can
Wheelbarrow

Materials for Constructive and Creative Work and Investigation

Abacus
Adding-machine tape
Adhesives of all varieties
Aerators
Aluminum foil
Alabastine
Aprons
Arches
Atlas
Attribute blocks
Balance, standard
Balance with arm fitted with
  hooks
Balance with movable arm to
  vary length on either side of
  pivot point
Ball bearings
Balloons
Ballpoint pens
Balsa wood
Bandage
Basins
Bathroom scales
Batteries
Beans
Bellows
Bicycle
Bicycle pump
Binoculars
Bird table
Black paper
Blotting paper
Blue bag
Bolts
Books
Bottles; glass, polyethylene,
  squeezy, stoppered
Bottletops

Bowls
Boxes, all sizes from pill box to
    show box
Brick salt
Broom handles
Bubble pipes
Buckets
Bulb holders
Bulbs
Bulldog clips
Buttons
Calendars
Calipers
Camera
Candles
Cane body clay
Carbon paper
Cardboard cones, as used in
    spinning mills
Cardboard tubes
Cardboard of varying
    thicknesses
Cartons
Cellophane envelopes
Chain 22 yards long
Chalk
Charcoal
Checkers sets
Chess sets
Chocolate wrappings
Clay bins
Clay tools
Clay trays
Clinical thermometer
Clock
Clock spring
Clothes brush
Clothes pegs
Cloves ·
Coarse sand; care must be taken
    to see that it does not contain
    lime

Cochineal
Coils
Coins
Colander
Collecting trays
Colored pencils
Colored ink
Color factor structured apparatus
Color filters
Compass
Concave mirrors
Cones
Conkers
Connector
Convex mirrors
Cooking oil
Cooking thermometer
Copthorne arch
Cork board
Corks
Corn
Corrugated card
Cotton reels
Cotton wool
Crayons
Cubes
Cuboid
Cuisenaire structural apparatus
Cylinders
Detergent
Dictionaries
Dienes AEM Material
Dienes MAB Material
Dog biscuits
Dominoes
Dowelling
Drinking straws
Dyes
Egg cartons
Egg timers
Elastic
Elastic bands

Elastic yarn
Electrical gear
Electrical wire
Electric bell
Electric motor
Embroidery silks
Equalizer
Expanded polystyrene, all sizes
Fablon
Fabrics
Feathers
Felt
Felt pens
Ferroplate mirrors
Fiddle frames
Filter paper
Flex
Florists' wire
Flour
Flower pots
Foam rubber
Food coloring
Football bladders
Frieze paper
Funnels
Fur
Gardening tools
Gauze
Geoboards
Geographical globe
Geometric shapes
Geometric shapes for filling
Glass beads
Gloving needles
Glycerine
Golf tees
Graph paper
Gravel
Greaseproof paper
Greyboard
Grouping sets
Gummed flint squares

Gyroscopes
Hardboard offcuts
H blocks
Health salts
Height measure
Hessian
Hex game
Home-made books
Hose pipe
Hundred square
Insect cages
Insulating tape
Iron filings
Jam jars
Jigsaw puzzles
Jugs
Junk boxes
Kaleidoscope
Kettle
Keys
Kitchen scales, spring
Kitchen scales with weights
Kite
Knitting pins
Lace
Laths
Lead shot
Leather
Leather offcuts
Leather punch
Lego
Lenses of all kinds
Lentils
Line
Liquid measures
Locks
Logic blocks
Logs
Loofahs
Madison project cards
Magnetic board
Magnets of all sizes and shapes

Magnet wire
Magnifiers, all types
Magnifying glasses
Maps
Marbles
Matador
Material, man-made and natural
    fibers
Materials for mosaics
Mechanical egg whisk
Mechanical junk
Medicine droppers
Metals, all kinds and weights
Meteorological equipment
Methylated spirit burner
Metronome
Micrometer
Microscope
Minerals
Mirrors of all types
Modelling tools
Morse key
Mosaic shapes
Moulds
Mustard
Nail brush
Needles with wooden handles
Needlework paper
Net
Newspaper
Nightlights
Nuts and bolts
Nylon line
Old clocks
Olive oil
Packing paper
Paint brushes
Paint diffusers
Painting paper
Palettes
Paper clips

Paper fasteners
Paper for books
Paper punch
Paraffin wax
Paste brushes
Pastels
Pattern paper
Patty tins
Peas
Pebbles
Peg board
Pencil sharpener
Pendulum frame
Pendulums
Pentominoes
Pets
Phrase strips
Pinger
Pins
Pipe cleaners
Plankton nets
Plaster of Paris
Plastic cake containers
Plasticine
Plastic Meccano
Plastic windmills
Plastitak
Plates
Playing cards
Plot of garden
Plot of rough ground
Poleidoblocs, colored and plain
Polyfilla
Polymer paint
Polystyrene balls
Polyethylene bags, small
Polyethylene tubes
Poster paint
Potatoes
Powder paint
Press studs

Printing ink
Prisms
Pulleys, double and single
Quoits
Red clay
Reference books with authentic
   pictures and information
Resin-based paint
Rheostats
Ribbon
Rice
Rigid plastic tubing
Rock salt
Room thermometer
Rope
Rubber tubing
Safety pins
Salt
Sawdust
Scales
Scissors
Scrabble
Screwdrivers
Sealing wax
Seeds
Seesaw balance on a fulcrum
Sellotape
Sequins
Sewing cotton
Sewing needles
Shells
Silver sand
Skittles
Slides
Slinky
Snails
Snakes and ladders
Snap cards
Soap flakes
Soda
Soft iron U bends

Spinning tops
Spirit level
Sponges
Spools
Spoons, graded sizes
Sprayers
Spring balances
Springs
Squared paper
Stapler
Stern arithmetic apparatus
Stones
Stopwatch
Storybooks
Straight edge
Straight tubing
Straw
String
Sugar
Sugar paper
Switches
Table tennis balls
Tape
Tape measures
Table covering
Table salt
Teapot
Tea strainers
Ten-second timer
Terylene line
Test tube rack
Test tubes
Textured paper
Thick lead pencils
Think-a-dot
Thin lead pencils
Three-dimensional tic-tac-toe
Timberlay
Timetables
Tin lids
Tins

Tissue paper, all colors
Toilet roll centers
Torches
Tower of Hanoi
Toys such as cars, animals,
     birds, furniture, utensils
Transistor radio
Transparent flexible tubing of
     various diameters
Transparent plastic hosepipe
Trays
Trundle wheels
Turntable
U-shaped tubing
Vacuum cleaner
Velvet
Vinegar
Vivarium
Wall paper
Wall paper sample books
Washers
Washing powder
Washing-up liquid
Water containers
Watering can with different
     sized roses
Weights
Wheelbarrow
Wheels
White plastic dishes
Wire
Wood
Wooden balls, various sizes
Wooden beads
Wooden spades
Wooden spoons
Wood files, round and triangular
Wood shavings
Wormery
X-Acto knife
X Blocks

APPENDIX C
ACTION
FOR
CHILDREN'S
TELEVISION—
A
CHRONOLOGY

This charts the development of the foremost advocacy group concerned with children and television.

January 1968 Informal meetings, discussions and research concerning children's television. Aims clarified.

Spring 1969 Monitoring of *Romper Room* for four weeks. Petition circulated protesting host selling and using child participants to demonstrate products. Met with station and program producers at WHDH, Boston.

February 5, 1970 Met with six of seven Federal Communications Commissioners to talk about need for overall regulation of children's TV and to present petition to eliminate ads from children's programs.

Spring 1970 ACT files briefs with FCC on ACT Petition. Support sought by ACT from public and national organizations.

March 1970 ACT commissions study "Programming and Advertising Practices in Television Directed to Children" by Ralph Jennings.

ATC commissions pilot study "Mother's Attitudes Toward Children's Television Programs and Commercials" by Daniel Yankelovitch, Inc. Both studies submitted as part of ACT filing to FCC.

October 15, 16, 1970 First national Symposium on Children and Television co-hosted by ACT, Kennedy Memorial Hospital for Children, and Boston University School of Public Communications, at the Kennedy Hospital.

May 1971   ACT commissions study "Saturday Morning Children's Programming on Boston TV Stations, May–June 1971" by Professor F. Earle Barcus of Boston University School of Public Communications.

Summer 1971   ACT opens office at 46 Austin Street, Newtonville, Massachusetts 02160.

October 18, 1971   Second National Symposium on Children and Television, co-sponsored with American Academy of Pediatrics at Palmer House Hotel, Chicago.

December 1971   ACT files petition with FTC to prohibit selling of toys to children on TV.

March 1972   ACT testifies at hearings on the Surgeon General's Report on Television and Social Behavior conducted by Senator John Pastore.

ACT files petition with FTC to prohibit selling of edibles to children on TV.

April 1972   ACT files specific complaints with the FTC against three major drug companies for advertising vitamins directly to children.

July 1972   Three major drug companies agree to end advertising for vitamin pills on children's commercial TV programs in response to ACT's petition. (FTC has not yet acted.)

October 1972   Third National Symposium on Children and Television in cooperation with the Yale Child Study Center and the Yale School of Art and Architecture, New Haven.

First informal meeting of ACT Contacts from across the country.

ACT commissions pilot study by BEST (Black Efforts for Soul in Television) analyzing treatment of Black and other minority groups on network children's television.

January 1973   National Association of Broadcasters initiates new code rules: (1) Banning host selling on children's television and (2) reducing commercial minutes on weekend children's schedules to 12.

March 1973   ACT files specific complaints with FTC against cereal and candy companies and CBS-TV Network for TV advertising of sugared edibles directed to children, and files supplement to edibles petition.

ACT files a brief with the FTC on proposed guides advocating the prohibition of endorsements and testimonials in advertisements aimed at children.

Fall 1973　ACT-commissioned study, "Children's Television: The Economics of Exploitation," by Dr. William H. Melody, is published by Yale University Press.

March 1974　ACT and other consumer representatives submit to the FTC a compromise code of guidelines for children's advertising. Industry calls compromise unacceptable.

April 1974　ACT holds its fourth annual conference, an international Festival of Children's Television, at the Kennedy Center for the Performing Arts in Washington, D.C.

June 1974　In response to ACT pressure, the Television Code Review Board of the National Association of Broadcasters recommends that by December 31 the amount of commercial time be cut from 12 to 10 minutes per hour, and to 9½ minutes per hour on weekends by 1975.

September 1974　ACT submits comments to the FTC on Proposed Guidelines Concerning Use of Premiums on Television Advertisements Directed to Children.

October 1974　Pantheon publishes ACT's *The Family Guide to Children's Television: What to Watch, What to Miss, What to Change, and How to Do It,* by Evelyn Kaye Sarson, former executive director of ACT.

November 1974　FCC issues Report and Policy Statement on Children's Television Programs but fails to issue any rules.

February 1975　ACT files lawsuit charging FTC inaction on food advertising petition, in U.S. District Court, Washington, D.C.

June 1975　In response to an ACT request, WDCA-TV, an independent television station in Washington, D.C., withdraws a two-week series of 54 fireworks commercials scheduled to air on afternoon and early-evening children's programs prior to July 4.

October 1975　ACT files a petition for rulemaking with the FTC to prohibit the advertising of vitamins on children's and family television programs. As part of the filing, ACT registers a formal complaint and request for injunctive relief against Hudson Pharmaceutical Corporation, manufacturer of Spiderman Vitamins.

November 1975　ACT holds its Fifth National Symposium on Children and Television, "Children's Television and the Arts," at the Memorial Arts Center in Atlanta.

ACT files a brief for an appeal of the FCC Policy Statement on Children's TV in the U.S. Court of Appeals in Washington, D.C.

December 1975 ACT releases "Weekend Commercial Children's Television" and "Television in the Afterschool Hours," studies by Dr. F. Earle Barcus dealing with children's TV programming on network and independent stations.

February 1976 In response to ACT's complaints about a series of fireworks ads which were scheduled on WDCA-TV, the NAB Code Review Board voted to ban all televised fireworks advertising effective February 1, 1976.

March 1976 ACT and the NCCB file an *amicus curiae* brief critical of the Family Hour, supporting the Writers' Guild of America, West, in its suit against the FCC and the networks on this issue.

May 1976 ACT files a formal complaint with the FTC against Mars, Inc., for its prominently advertised Milky Way commercial, which advocates a child's consumption of the candy bar "wherever you are . . . at work, rest, or play."

ACT participates in a joint FCC–FTC panel on the advertising of over-the-counter drugs on television.

September 1976 ACT releases "Pre-Christmas Advertising to Children," a study by Dr. F. Earle Barcus comparing advertising on children's TV programs broadcast in April and November 1975.

Responding to ACT's formal complaint against Hudson Pharmaceutical Corp., the FTC issues a consent order prohibiting the company from "directing its advertising for Spiderman and other children's vitamins to child audiences."

Oral argument in ACT's suit against the FCC is presented before the U.S. Court of Appeals in Washington by attorneys Earle K. Moore and Henry Geller.

ACT is cited in Ann Landers' syndicated newspaper column and receives over 25,000 inquiries seeking information concerning violence on children's television.

October 1976 ACT receives the American Academy of Pediatrics Distinguished Public Service Award.

November 1976 U.S. District Judge Warren J. Ferguson of Los Angeles Federal Court supports ACT's contention by ruling that the Family Viewing Hour violates the First Amendment.

ACT holds its Sixth National Symposium on Children and Television, "Products and Programs: The Child as Consumer," in Cambridge in cooperation with the Harvard Graduate School of Education.

December 1976 ACT files a complaint with the FTC against Hasbro Industries, Inc., for using deceptive practices to advertise its Bulletman toy in television commercials directed at children.

April 1977 ACT files petition with FTC to prohibit the advertising of candy to children on television.

May 1977 ACT announces publication of its resource book, *Promise and Performance: ACT's Guide to TV Programming for Children, Volume I: Children with Special Needs.*

June 1977 ACT files formal complaint with the Federal Trade Commission against General Foods Corporation for its TV commercials for Cocoa Pebbles.

July 1977 Federal Trade Commission Chairman Michael Pertschuk meets with ACT and 14 national groups on proposed regulation of TV candy ads.

August 1977 ACT files formal FTC complaint against Ralston Purina's advertising campaign for Cookie Crisp, a presweetened cereal.

November 1977 ACT holds a research workshop on "Televised Role Models and Young Adolescents" at the Harvard Graduate School of Education. FTC Chairman Michael Pertschuk is a featured speaker.

February 1978 ACT files petition with the Federal Communications Commission to ultimately eliminate all advertising from children's TV programs.

The Federal Trade Commission initiates a rulemaking procedure which will consider the elimination of TV advertising directed to children under eight and a ban on ads for highly sugared snacks directed to children under twelve.

May 1978 ACT holds its Seventh National Symposium, "TV Role Models and Young Adolescents," in Washington, D.C., in cooperation with George Washington University.

June 1978 ACT publishes "Commercial Television on Weekends and Weekday Afternoons," a monitoring study by Dr. F. Earle Barcus analyzing programming and advertising broadcast during October 1977 on the three networks and on independent stations in Boston and elsewhere.

July 1978 On July 27 the FCC initiates a new inquiry into children's advertising and programming practices in order to study voluntary compliance by broadcasters with the 1974 Children's Television Report and Policy Statement.

November 1978 ACT holds a conference "Act on the Arts: Television, the Arts and Young People" in New York City. The meeting was the first in a series of regional workshops designed to encourage innovative arts programming for children on local television.

ACT files almost 1,000 pages of legal comment and supporting studies with the FTC in Washington as the official record in the children's television rulemaking closes. Preparation begins for hearings scheduled for March 1979.

January 1979 ACT files comments with the FCC in the Second Notice of Inquiry on Children's Programming and Advertising Practices and requests the commission to initiate a rulemaking proceeding to remedy the failures of industry self-regulation.

January and March 1979 Thirteen witnesses testify on behalf of ACT at the Federal Trade Commission hearings on television advertising to children.

February 1979 ACT premieres new film *Kids for Sale: A Look at Commercial Television.*

ACT petitions the U.S. Consumer Product Safety Commission to regulate the safety and design of projectile toys, stating that industry self-regulation has failed to protect children.

April 1979 ACT files comments supporting a petition that adolescent television programming be reported on the FCC license renewal form, on grounds that this would stimulate more programming for this segment of the viewing audience.

May 1979 ACT announces seventh annual "Achievement in Children's Television" Awards.

ACT announces publication of the revised edition of *The ACT Guide to Children's Television: How to Treat TV with T.L.C.*

June 1979   ACT begins first nationwide public-service radio campaign, designed to inform and educate listeners about the influence of television on children.

ACT files a brief with the Federal Trade Commission proposing issues in the rulemaking on children's advertising which remain in dispute and should be resolved in further hearings.

July 1979   ACT submits statements to the House and Senate Communications Subcommittees regarding the proposed rewrite of the Communications Act of 1934, urging specifically that the public-interest standard be retained in any revision of the present law.

July 1979   FTC Presiding Officer recommends that three issues in the children's advertising rulemaking be examined further in disputed issues hearings.

September 1979   ACT hosts a second symposium, "ACT on the Arts: Television, the Arts and Young People," in Minneapolis.

ACT files with the FCC a letter supporting a petition seeking rules limiting the amount of commercial time permitted during children's and adults' television programs.

ACT announces publication of its second resource book, *Promise and Performance: ACT's Guide to TV Programming for Children, Volume II: The Arts.*

ACT is invited to testify before the Senate Consumer Subcommittee.

ACT urges the members of Congress to authorize the FTC to continue the children's advertising rulemaking proceeding, citing the broad public support for the inquiry.

October 1979   The FCC Task Force on Children's Television reports to the commission that broadcasters have failed to meet their obligations to improve children's television programming.

December 1979   ACT files comments with the FCC on the Children's Television Task Force Report and urges the commission to initiate a rulemaking proceeding.

The Federal Communications Commission votes to adopt a rulemaking procedure on children's television programming.

APPENDIX D
LOCAL CHILDREN'S TELEVISION COMMITTEES

Atlanta Council for Children's
Television
P.O. Box 52742
Atlanta, GA 30355

Baltimore Media Alliance
P.O. Box 16262
Baltimore, MD 21210

Colorado Committee on
Children's Television
P.O. Box 663
Englewood, CO 80151

Committee on Children's
Television
1511 Masonic Ave.
San Francisco, CA 94117

Citizens for Better Television
5811 Woodland Road
Des Moines, IA 50312

Committee for Children's
Television of Metro Detroit
2338 N. Woodward
Royal Oak, MI 48073

Dayton Area Council for
Children's Television
988 Oakwood Ave.
Dayton, OH 45419

Kalamazoo Committee for
Children's Television
5228 Ridgebrook Drive
Portage, MI 49081

Lancaster Organization on Kids'
TV
519 North School Lane
Lancaster, PA 17603

Lansing Committee for
Children's Television
1002 N. Foster
Lansing, MI 48912

Los Angeles Coalition on
Children and Television
10906 Rochester Ave.
Los Angeles, CA 90024

New York Council on Children's
Television
212 E. 77 St., Apt. 2C
New York, NY 10021

Pittsburgh Conference on
Children's Television
1420 Walnut St.
Pittsburgh, PA 15218

Puget Sound Action for
Children's Television

P.O. Box 99
Mercer Island, WA 98040

Rochester Coalition for
Children's Television
48-B Manor Parkway
Rochester, NY 14620

Washington Association for
Television and Children
4418 MacArthur Blvd., N.W.
Suite 202
Washington, DC 20007

Foreign Committees

The Australian Children's
Television Action Committee

70 Aberdeen Road
Mac Leod, Victoria, Australia
3085

Forum for Children's Television
c/o Midori F. Suzuki
Nagae 1601-27
Hayama-cho
Kanagawa-Ken, Japan

The Children's Television
Committee
Mejor Television Para Ninos
Sevilla 1016, Col. Portales
Mexico 13, D.F.

APPENDIX E
NATIONAL RESEARCH AND REFORM GROUPS

Action For Children's Television (ACT)
46 Austin Street
Newtonville, MA 02160

Media Action Research Center, Inc. (MARC)
475 Riverside Drive
Suite 1370
New York, NY 10027

National Association for Better Broadcasting (NABB)
P.O. Box 43640
Los Angeles, CA 90043

National Citizen's Committee for Broadcasting (NCCB)
1028 Connecticut Avenue NW
Washington, DC 20036

National Council For Children and Television
20 Nassau Street
Princeton, NJ 08540

Office of Communication of the United Church of Christ
289 Park Avenue South
New York, NY 10010

The Yale University Family Television Research and Consultation Center
Dept. of Psychology, Yale University
Box 11A, Yale Station,
New Haven, CT 06520

RECOMMENDED SOURCES

BOOKS

Barnouw, Erik, *The Sponsor*. New York: Oxford University Press, 1978.

Barnouw, Erik, *The Tube of Plenty*. New York: Oxford University Press, 1975.

Bellak, Leopold, *Overload*. New York: Human Sciences Press, 1975.

Bettelheim, Bruno, *The Uses of Enchantment: The Meaning and Importance of Fairy Tales*. New York: Alfred A. Knopf, 1976.

Broadman, Muriel, *Understanding Your Child's Entertainment*. New York: Harper & Row, 1977.

Brown, Les, *Keeping Your Eye on Television*. New York: Pilgrim Press, 1979.

Brown, Les, *The New York Times Encyclopedia of Television*. New York: Times Books, 1980.

Brown, Les, *Television: The Business Behind the Box*. New York: Harcourt Brace Jovanovich, 1971.

Brown, Les, and Marks, Selma, *Electric Media*. New York: Harcourt Brace Jovanovich, 1974.

Carnegie Commission on the Future of Public Broadcasting, *A Public Trust*. New York: Bantam Books, 1979.

Channeling Children: Sex Stereotyping on Prime Time TV. An analysis by Women on Words and Images. Princeton, N.J., 1975.

Cohen, Dorothy H., *The Learning Child*. New York: Vintage Books, 1973.

Cohen, Dorothy H., and Rudolph, Marguerita, *Kindergarten and Early Schooling*. Englewood Cliffs, N.J.: Prentice Hall, 1977.

Cohen, Dorothy H. and Stern, Virginia, *Observing and Recording the Behavior of Young Children*. New York: Teachers College Press, Teachers College, Columbia Univ., 1978.

Comstock, George, et. al., *Television and Human Behavior*. New York: Columbia University Press, 1978.

Doing the Media: A Portfolio of Activities and Resources, Laybourne, Kit, ed. New York: The Center for Understanding Media, 1972.

Edwards, Betty, *Drawing on the Right Side of the Brain*. New York: St. Martin's Press, 1979.

223

Goldsen, Rose K., *The Show and Tell Machine.* New York: Dell Publishing, 1978.

Kaye, Evelyn, *The ACT Family Guide to Children's Television.* Boston: Beacon Press, 1979.

Keniston, Kenneth, and the Carnegie Council on Children, *All Our Children.* New York and London: Harcourt Brace Jovanovich, 1977.

Lesser, Gerald, *Children and Television—Lessons from Sesame Street.* New York: Random House, 1974.

Liebert, Robert M., Neale, John M., and Davidson, Emily S., *The Early Window—Effects of Television on Children and Youth.* New York: Pergamon Press, 1973.

Mander, Jerry, *Four Arguments for the Elimination of Television.* New York: William Morrow, 1978.

Masters, Robert, and Houston, Jean, *Listening To the Body.* New York: Delacorte Press, 1978.

Melody, William, *Children's Television: The Economics of Exploitation.* New Haven and London: Yale University Press, 1973.

Murray, Michael, *The Videotape Book.* New York: Bantam Books, 1975.

Postman, Neil, *Teaching as a Conserving Activity.* New York: Delacorte Press, 1979.

Potter, Rosemary Lee, *New Season: The Positive Use of Commercial Television with Children.* Columbus, Ohio: Charles E. Merrill Publishing Company, 1976.

Promise and Performance: Children with Special Needs—ACT's guide to TV programming for children, Maureen Harmonay, ed. Cambridge, Mass: Ballinger Publishing Co., 1977.

Schwartz, Tony, *The Responsive Chord.* New York: Anchor Press/Doubleday, 1973.

Singer, Dorothy G., and Singer, Jerome L., *Partners in Play—A Step-by-Step Guide to Imaginative Play.* New York: Harper & Row, 1977.

Singer, Jerome L., *The Child's World of Make-Believe.* New York: Academic Press, 1973.

Television Awareness Training, Logan, Ben, and Moody, Kate, ed. New York: A Media Action Research Center (MARC) publication, 1979.

United States Commission on Civil Rights, *Window Dressing on the Set: An Update.* Washington, D.C.: U.S. Government Printing Office, 1979.

Ward, Scott, Wackman, Daniel B., and Wartella, Ellen, *How Children Learn to Buy.* Beverly Hills, Calif.: Sage Press, 1977.

Winn, Marie, *The Plug-In Drug—Television and the Family*. New
York: Viking Press, 1977.
Winn, Marie, and Porcher, Mary Ann, *The Playgroup Book*. New
York: Macmillan, 1967.

FILMS

These films are designed to promote adult awareness of the effects of
television on children.

It's as Easy as Selling Candy to a Baby. This film shows the effects of
TV on the health and buying habits of young children; specific data
on effects of sugar consumption. Fifteen minutes. Action for
Children's Television, 46 Austin St., Newtonville, MA 02160.
Kids for Sale. Most highly recommended film for adult groups. This
film looks at the discrepancies between what children's television
is and what it could be; it explores the effects of television
commercials, stereotyping, and violence on young viewers. Twenty
minutes, color, 16 mm. Rental, $30 from Action for Children's
Television, 46 Austin St., Newtonville, MA 02160.
TV: The Anonymous Teacher. Designed for parents, teachers, and
community, this 15-minute film includes interviews with psychologists, parents, and other specialists on the influence of TV. In
color, 16 mm. Rental, $20 from Mass Media Ministries, 2116 N.
Charles St., Baltimore, MD 21218.

PERIODICALS

access. National Citizen's Committee for Broadcasting, 1028 Connect-
icut Ave., Room 402, Washington, DC 20036 Biweekly. $24.00/year.
Journal of Communication. Annenberg School of Communications,
P.O. Box 13358, Philadelphia, PA 19101. Quarterly. $15.00/year.
NCCT Forum. National Council for Children and Television, 20
Nassau St., Suite 215, Princeton, NJ 08540. Quarterly.
re:act. Action for Children's Television, 46 Austin St., Newtonville,
MA 02160. Quarterly. $15.00/year.
Young Viewers. Media Center for Children/Children's Film Theater,
43 West 61 St., New York, NY 10023. Quarterly.

NOTES

1. GROWING UP ON TELEVISION

1. Statistics about TV technology and viewing habits have been obtained from the Television Information Office (TIO), the A.C. Nielsen Co., both in New York, and the Electronics Institute of America in Washington, D.C.

2. Survey data gathered for the Surgeon General's Report (1972) showed that it is *parents* who consciously promote the viewing of *Sesame* by young children, believing that it is somehow a basic element in their education. *Sesame*, to a greater extent than other quality programs for children, had the underlying effect of legitimizing TV viewing by children in the minds of adults and communicating the general notion that "TV is good for children."

2. THE PHYSICAL EFFECTS

1. In his book, *Four Arguments for the Elimination of Television* (New York: William Morrow, 1978), Jerry Mander reports the work of Dr. Erik Peper, Dr. Thomas Mulholland, and Drs. Merrelyn and Fred Emery. In addition, I have reviewed the published material and discussed numerous remaining questions with researchers in this field. If you are not put off by the title of Mander's book, you will find important material which is often highly entertaining, such as the chapter titled "The Ingestion of Artificial Light."

2. See Dr. T. Berry Brazelton's article, "How to Tame the TV Monster," *Redbook*, April 1972.

3. See *The Lancet*, October 31, 1970, for a letter to the editor by P. M. Jeavons and G.F.A. Harding.

4. See "Self-induced Television Epilepsy" by Pierre Clement, *Canadian Psychiatric Association Journal*, Vol. 21, No. 3, 1976.

5. See "Turned on Toddlers" by Werner I. Halpern, M.D., *Journal of Communication*, Autumn 1975, published by the Annenberg School of Communication, the University of Pennsylvania.

6. Much of the information on eye movements and TV viewing was obtained from unpublished papers, notes, and interviews with Dr. Edgar Gording, Clinical Director of the Gording Clinic for Developmental Vision, 1100 Graham Ave., Windber, Pa.

7. From an unpublished paper by Dr. Edgar Gording and Kathleen

Lewis, "Television and Visual Dysfunction—Multi-Microstrabismus."

8. For a broad discussion of the diverse effects of microwaves, see *The Zapping of America—Microwaves: Their Deadly Risk and the Cover-up* by Paul Brodeur, New York: W.W. Norton, 1977.

9. See *Health and Light* by Dr. John Ott, Greenwich, Conn.: Devin-Adair Company, 1973.

3. THE EFFECTS ON LEARNING AND PERCEPTION

1. Report of research by Michael Morgan and Larry Gross, both of the Annenberg School of Communications at the University of Pennsylvania, titled, "Reading, Writing and Watching: Television Viewing, IQ and Academic Achievement." Financed by a grant from the National Institute of Mental Health (NIMH), this research was part of the Cultural Indicators Project at the Annenberg School.

2. See Arnold Gesell and Frances Ilg's *Infant and Child in the Culture of Today*, New York: Harper Brothers, 1943.

3. See Dorothy Cohen and Marguerita Rudolph's *Kindergarten and Early Schooling*, Englewood Cliffs, N.J.: Prentice-Hall, 1977.

4. From remarks by David Sontag of Prime-Time Television (Twentieth Century Fox) at ACT convention, 1978, in Washington, D.C.

5. Reported in *Children and the Worlds of Television: A Cognitive Developmental Study*—a part of Harvard's Project Zero report to the John and Mary R. Markle Foundation, 1977.

6. See Walter Lippmann's *Public Opinion*, New York: Macmillan, 1960.

7. George Gerbner and his colleagues published these findings in "Cultural Indicators: Violence Profile No. 9," *Journal of Communication*, Summer 1978, published by the Annenberg School of Communications, the University of Pennsylvania.

8. This survey was released by the Foundation for Child Development in New York in 1977.

9. See *Window Dressing on the Set: An Update*, a report of the U.S. Commission on Civil Rights, January 1979.

10. See Dorothy Cohen's "Is TV a Pied Piper?" *Young Children*, November 1974.

11. See Dorothy and Jerome Singer's *Partners in Play*, New York: Harper and Row, 1977, for an expanded discussion of the role of imagination in child development, including ways to enhance its growth.

12. Reported in Jerome Singer's *The Child's World of Make-Believe: Experimental Studies of Imaginative Play*, New York: Academic Press, 1973.

13. Erik Barnouw discusses what he understands to be "absorption in the symbolic process" in his book, *The Sponsor—Notes on a Modern Potentate*, New York: Oxford University Press, 1978, and in *The Image Empire*, New York: Oxford University Press, 1970.

14. Reported by Dorothy Singer in "Television and Imaginative Play," *Journal of Mental Imagery*, 2, 1978.

4. THE EFFECTS ON READING

1. Numerous studies across the years have documented this fact. See Dolores Durkin's "Children Who Read Before Grade 1: A Second Study," *Elementary School Journal*, 64, 1963. See also Esther Milner's "A Study of the Relationship Between Reading Readiness in Grade One School Children and Patterns of Parent–Child Interaction," *Child Development*, 22, 1951.

2. See Maya Pines, *Revolution in Learning—the Years from Birth*, New York: Harper and Row, 1967.

3. See "The Effect of Literature on Vocabulary and Reading Achievement" by Dorothy H. Cohen, *Elementary English*, February 1968.

4. See "Television Language and Book Language" by Adele Morgan Fasick, *Elementary School English*, February 1973.

5. THE PROMOTION OF AGGRESSIVE BEHAVIOR

1. See content analysis by Rita Wickes Poulos, Susan E. Harvey, and Robert M. Liebert, *Saturday Morning Television: A Profile of the 1974–75 Children's Season*, New York: Media Action Research Center (MARC), 1976.

2. Reported by Les Brown in *Television: The Business Behind the Box*, New York: Harcourt Brace Jovanovitch, 1973.

3. See *War and Children* by Anna Freud and Dorothy T. Burlingham, London: Medical War Books, 1943.

4. Many studies on observational learning exist, such as those by Alberta Siegel, Hilde Himmelweit, Robert Liebert, George Gerbner, and others which are reported in The Surgeon General's Report; *Television and Human Behavior* by George Comstock, New York: Columbia University Press, 1978; and *The Early Window* by Robert

M. Liebert, John M. Neale, and Emily S. Davidson, Elmsford, N.Y., Pergamon Press, 1973. The earliest work however was by Albert Bandura, D. Ross, and I. A. Ross and was reported in "Imitation of Film-Mediated Aggressive Models," *Journal of Abnormal and Social Psychology*, 67, 1963.

5. See the Surgeon General's Scientific Advisory Committee on Television and Social Behavior report titled *Television and Growing Up: The Impact of Televised Violence*, 5 vols., Washington, D.C.: U.S. Government Printing Office, 1972.

6. See *Growing Up to be Violent—A Longitudinal Study of the Development of Aggression*, by Monroe M. Lefkowitz, Leonard D. Eron, Leopold O. Walder, L. Rowell Huesmann, Elmsford, N.Y.: Pergamon Press, Inc., 1977.

7. Aimee Dorr reported these findings in a paper, "Contexts for Behavior in Television Programs and Children's Subsequent Behavior," presented at the biennial meeting of the Society for Research in Child Development in Philadelphia, 1973.

6. THE EFFECTS ON HEALTH AND LIFE-STYLE

1. Described in *Advertising Age*, July 19, 1965.

2. See "Children's Programming," in Les Brown's *New York Times Encyclopedia of Television*, New York: Quadrangle, 1977. Other entries in the encyclopedia are recommended for the overall study of children and television, including "Children's Advertising," "Children's Television Policy Statement," "Children's Television Workshop," "Broadcast Reform Movement," "Television, Technology of," "Television Code," "Action for Children's Television," and more.

3. These statistics are from the research of Robert Choate of the Council on Children, Media & Merchandising based in Washington, D.C. Choate has been one of the persistent advocates for children in the drawn-out policy discussions on nutrition and TV.

4. Toy prices based on local retail prices in the New England area in September 1978 and on prices in leading mail-order catalogs, compiled by ACT.

5. Interview with a vice-president of Ideal Toy Co. at Harvard University, 1976.

6. Reported in *Kids, Food and Television: The Compelling Case for State Action* by Frank Mauro and Roberta Feins, published by the New York State Assembly, 1977.

7. See "Too Much Sugar?" in *Consumer Reports*, March 1978.

8. See Adelle Davis's *Let's Have Healthy Children*, New York: New American Library, 1972.

9. See B. F. Feingold's *Why Your Child is Hyperactive*, New York: Random House, 1975.

10. Joan Gussow is a nutrition educator, currently chairperson of the Department of Nutrition at Teachers College, Columbia University, New York.

11. See "Young Viewers' Troubling Response to TV Ads" by T. G. Bever, M. D. Smith, B. Bengen, and T. G. Johnson, *Harvard Business Review*, November 1975.

7. THE EFFECTS ON SOCIAL RELATIONSHIPS

1. See Dr. Chester Pierce's article, "An Experiment in Racism," in *Education and Urban Society*, November 1977.

2. Joyce Sprafkin has written extensively on this subject. For more of her findings, see "Stereotyping and TV," in *Television Awareness Training*, New York: Media Action Research Center, 1979.

3. See *Window Dressing on the Set; An Update*, a study by the U.S. Civil Rights Commission, 1979.

4. See F. Earle Barcus's analysis, *Commercial Children's Television on Weekends and Weekday Afternoons*, Newtonville, Mass.: Action for Children's Television, 1978.

5. This and other information on sexual stereotypes was drawn from several sources, in particular: *Channeling Children: Sex Stereotyping on Prime Time TV*, an analysis by Women on Words and Images, 1975; and *Window Dressing on the Set: An Update*, a study by the U.S. Civil Rights Commission, 1979.

6. See "Young People and Social Television Learning" by Charles Atkin and Bradley Greenberg, in *Televised Role Models and Young Adolescents: An ACT Research Workshop*, Newtonville, Mass.: Action for Children's Television, 1977.

7. See Brenda Grayson's article, "Television and Minorities," in *Television Awareness Training—A Viewer's Guide*, New York: Media Action Research Center, 1979.

8. See *Commercial Children's Television on Weekends and Weekday Afternoons* by F. Earle Barcus, Newtonville, Mass.: Action for Children's Television, 1978; and *Window Dressing on the Set; An Update*, a study by the U.S. Civil Rights Commission, 1979.

9. See Dr. Chester Pierce's article, "An Experiment in Racism," in *Education in Urban Society*, November 1977.

10. The study, as well as the study on soap opera families, can be found in Rose Goldsen's book, *The Show and Tell Machine*, Dell Publishing, 1978.

11. Reported in "What Happened When 5 Families Stopped Watching TV?" in *Good Housekeeping*, September 1979.

12. See "Cultural Indicators: Violence Profile No. 9" by George Gerbner, Larry Gross, Marilyn Jackson-Beeck, Suzanne Jefferies-Fox, and Nancy Signorelli, *Journal of Communication*, Summer 1978.

13. This finding emerged in a survey by the Foundation for Child Development, New York, 1977.

14. See "Children and TV-Land" by Sherryl Graves, *Response*, March 1979.

8. ACTION AT THE HOME

1. Quoted in *Television Awareness Training—A Viewer's Guide*, New York: Media Action Research Center, 1979.

9. ACTION IN SCHOOL

1. Described by Rosemary Lee Potter in her book *New Season*, Columbus, Ohio: Charles E. Merrill Publishing Co., 1976. Reprinted by permission.

2. As reported in *TV Guide*, June 1979.

3. From the experience of Les Brown, as he reported it in his book (with Selma Marks) *Electric Media*, New York: Harcourt Brace Jovanovitch, 1974.

10. PUBLIC ACTION

1. Adapted from the article by Kate Moody, "Run for TV's School Board," *The Interpreter*, February 1978.

2. See *Children's Television: Economics of Exploitation* by William Melody, New Haven: Yale University Press, 1976.

INDEX

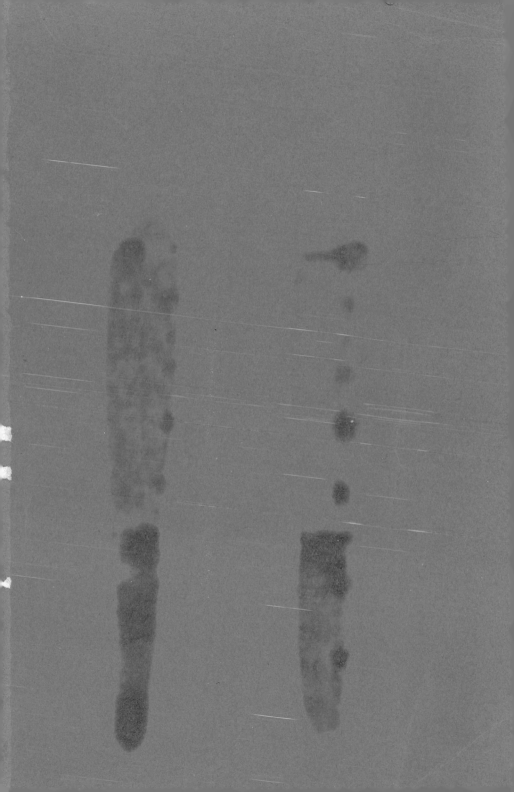